Praise from readers of the 'Secret

"These 'Secrets Exposed' books have truly h
and personal life since reading them. I found the ....
and I learnt something new from every contributor. I have recomm...
these books to many of my friends and I am looking forward to future
titles as I believe they will all hold secrets that will benefit me."

Sophie Kelsey – Budding businesswoman

"The 'Secrets Exposed' series has become my bible. A secret Rolodex to all
the most successful business minds. To be connected instantly to people
who are doing and have done what you dream and strive to become is
uplifting, inspiring and insightful."

Tania Menzies – Jelli Beanz International Nannies

"Huge congratulations on an absolutely fabulous read. I couldn't stop at one
book, I had to go out and get the entire 'Secrets Exposed' series. These books
are such an inspirational and practical read that I am telling everyone I know
to get them. If you want to create anything you would love in your life, go out
and get one. They won't just sit on your shelf, you'll turn to them regularly
for ideas, insights, and inspiration to create your own life dreams too. A small
investment to make to have a wealth of information at your fingertips."

Alison Nancye – The Mermaid Project

"This series were the first self-help books I ever read – before that I didn't
even know there was a 'self-help' section in the book store! They inspired
me and opened my eyes to all the things I can be. I now achieve many goals
– from not biting my fingernails to getting my Black Belt."

Kerstin Oberprieler – Student and 2nd Dan Taekwondo Black Belt

"I have read all four of the current 'Secrets Exposed' series, and can't wait for
the next editions. I find these books inspiring and insightful. Dale has created
something unique with all the wonderful 'added value' gifts throughout the
books, which I have enjoyed receiving and benefiting from."

Lee Clark – Customer Love

"The 'Secrets Exposed' series has been instrumental in allowing me to make a major mental shift about my business and sales. Each chapter is a separate inspiration and a clear reminder of the simple, daily action and persistence required to achieve success."

Nicole Seagren – VISION Finance Australia

"These 'Secrets Exposed 'books have taught me a lot more than I learnt during my studies. The practical information and tips have opened my eyes to new ways of doing things. In addition to the books, receiving the free downloads was like continuing that education. I am amazed at how much I have learnt!"

Brook York – Professional Athlete

"Secrets of Female Entrepreneurs Exposed! is undoubtedly the best investment I have ever made. I actually borrowed it twice from a library before I was able to purchase it. I needed to raise venture capital for my theatre company and reading how people were succeeding when others were saying 'don't', was inspiring. The 'Secrets Exposed' series is my mentor! Thank you to everyone for sharing your experience with me."

Rajendra Moodley – Elephanta Theatre Company

"I find myself continually referring to these books to recapture fleeting ideas or to buoy my own motivation when it ebbs below acceptable levels. The contributors' enthusiasm is contagious. I also found it fascinating reading about the evolution of their business ideas, many of which could be traced to some simple, seemingly innocuous, activity."

Sasha Dunn – Artist

SECRETS OF INSPIRING WOMEN EXPOSED!

$247
OF FREE
BONUS
GIFTS*

SECRETS OF INSPIRING WOMEN EXPOSED!

DALE BEAUMONT

WITH EMMA LYONS & FOREWORD BY LOUISE SAUVAGE

Disclaimer

All the information, techniques, skills and concepts contained within this publication are of the nature of general comment only, and are not in any way recommended as individual advice. The intent is to offer a variety of information to provide a wider range of choices now and in the future, recognising that we all have widely diverse circumstances and viewpoints. Should any reader choose to make use of the information contained herein, this is their decision, and the contributors (and their companies), authors and publishers do not assume any responsibilities whatsoever under any conditions or circumstances. It is recommended that the reader obtain their own independent advice.

FIRST EDITION 2007

Copyright © 2007 Dream Express International Pty Ltd

All rights reserved. No part of this publication may be reproduced, stored in a retrieval system, or transmitted in any form or by any means, electronic, mechanical, photocopying, recording or otherwise, without the prior written permission from the publisher.

National Library of Australia
Cataloguing-in-Publication entry:

Beaumont, Dale.
  Secrets of inspiring women exposed!

  1st ed.
  Includes index.
  ISBN 9780980308624.

  1. Women – Australia – Biography. 2. Successful people –
  Australia – Case studies. 3. Achievement motivation in
  women. I. Title. (Series: Secrets exposed).

305.40994

Published by Dream Express Publishing
A division of Dream Express International Pty Ltd
PO Box 567, Crows Nest, NSW 1585 Australia
Email: info@SecretsExposed.com.au
Website: www.SecretsExposed.com.au

Distributed in Australia by Gary Allen

For further information about orders:
Phone: +61 2 9725 2933
Email: customerservice@garyallen.com.au

Editing by Simone Tregeagle [simone@inkcommunications.com.au]
Layout and typesetting by Bookhouse [www.bookhouse.com.au]
Cover design by Jay Beaumont [www.thecreativehouse.com]
Illustrations by Grant Tulloch [info@secretsexposed.com.au]
Printed and bound by McPhersons Printing [www.mcphersonsprinting.com.au]

To a very special woman I call my nan. You have taught me so much – including how to sew a button back on my shirt and cook your very famous pancakes! Thanks for being such a beautiful soul and for giving me the book that started it all. Love you lots.

Dale Beaumont

To my mum and dad for their love and encouragement. To my family and friends for their endless support and to Pat, who truly was an inspiring woman and will always be in our hearts.

Emma Lyons

Acknowledgments

As with any major project, there are a number of very special people who contributed to making this book happen, so we'd like to take a short moment to say, 'Thank You'.

To the 13 delightful and extremely talented women featured in this book, the biggest *thank you* for accepting our invitation to be a part of this exciting project. It has been wonderful to learn from your journey and get a glimpse into how you impact the lives of everyone you meet.

To the wonderful Simone Tregeagle and Kerrin Medenyak (from Ink Communications) and Neil Murphy, our great editors – thank you so much for your ongoing support.

To Jay Beaumont (Dale's brother) for designing the book covers, to Bookhouse in Sydney who continue to do such excellent typesetting and to Robert Stapelfeldt – thanks for everything you do to bring all of the 'Secrets Exposed!' books to life.

Next, to Shaun Stenning and the rest of the team at Sure Fire Marketing. Thanks for all your efforts in the rebuilding of the 'Secrets Exposed!' website and for the ongoing web development. We really value your work and thank you for the many emails after midnight.

Thanks to all the staff at Gary Allen (our wonderful distributors) and each and every sales rep that has helped to get these books into the stores – we greatly appreciate the work you do.

And finally, to tens of thousands of readers that have supported the 'Secrets Exposed!' series – a very heartfelt thanks. May the words from our books continue to inspire and guide your way!

CONTENTS

PREFACE

If I were in your position right now I'd be wondering if I really needed to read this section. However, if this is the first 'Secrets Exposed!' book that you've read, could I ask you to please resist the temptation to skip ahead, as I'd like to briefly share with you why this book has been created and how you can best use it to impact your life.

When I was growing up I heard somewhere that there are two ways to live your life: the first is through 'trial and error' and the second is through 'other people's experience'. At the time I dismissed it as just another one of those sayings that sounds good, but doesn't make much sense. Then, like most teenagers I finished school with stars in my eyes thinking, 'This is great! My education is over – no more books, no more lectures, no more people telling me what to do'. How wrong I was. After a few months of bouncing around, not quite sure of what to do next, I stumbled across the idea of personal development and started to hear concepts such as:

- Formal education will earn you a living, but self-education will make you a fortune.
- Work harder on yourself than you do on your job.
- You will be the same person five years from now, except for the people you meet and the books you read.
- Don't wish that your job were easier, wish that you were better.
- You are your own greatest asset, so you must invest in yourself.

Since November 2000, I have been totally committed to becoming my own most valuable asset. After attending hundreds of seminars, listening to thousands of hours of CDs and reading shelves of books, I have discovered that the people who truly succeed aren't any smarter, better looking or harder working than anyone else – they just think differently and have learnt to incorporate different values into their lives.

I am now in the very fortunate position of being able to travel internationally to present personal development seminars to teenagers and I am often asked, 'What is the one thing you need to know to be successful?' My answer is always the same: 'The one thing that you need to know is that there is not *one* thing that you need to know to be successful'. I've learnt that success is multifaceted and that mastering one principle of success or area of your life isn't going to take you to the top – the more you master, the more successful you will become. But if I *did* have to identify one of the most important success strategies, it would be this: *'Find out what successful people do and do the same thing until you get the same results'*.

That's what this book is all about. The only difference is, instead of you going out and finding successful people, we've brought them to you.

You see, whatever you want in life, whatever you are shooting for, chances are that someone else is already living it. They have already invested years of their life and probably hundreds of thousands of dollars, they've made lots of mistakes, learnt from them and eventually succeeded. So why would you want to waste your own time, money and effort through 'trial and error' when you can fast-track your success by learning from 'someone else's experience'? As Sir Isaac Newton said, 'If I have seen further it is because I have been standing on the shoulders of giants'.

Every time you pick up a book, attend a seminar or interview a successful person, you are compressing years of life experience into a few hours. With any of the 'Secrets Exposed' books, you can multiply that by between twelve and seventeen people and you're looking at around 250+ years of experience and wisdom ready and waiting for you. It won't prevent you from making mistakes of your own, far from it, but it will help you to make more calculated and purposeful decisions, rather than big, misguided and ignorant ones.

There is no shortage of information about how to achieve proficiency or even greatness in any area of life these days. Go to any bookstore or library and you'll find the shelves sagging with titles from experts, all with their own theories and ways of doing things. But what I have discovered is lacking in almost all of these books is INSPIRATION. What's missing is role models and mentors – the stories of people we can all look up to. People who started out exactly like you – with a dream in their hearts and with all the same fears and insecurities. Given the choice between reading a textbook or a dozen success stories about people who have actually done something, I'd take the success stories any day of the week. I'm not saying that theoretical information isn't important, of course it is, but having presented hundreds of talks to all different types of audiences, I can confidently say that it's always the stories that move people. It's the whole, "If he or she did it, then so can I" that gets inside people's hearts. When we're inspired we get motivated and then we take positive action which leads to results.

The 'Secrets Exposed' books are not intended to be a one-stop-shop. They are an introduction to the wealth of knowledge available to you and to some of the real success stories of people who have reached the top in their chosen field of endeavour. That's why at the back of each book you will find most of the contributors' contact details and some of their other products and services that are available to help you continue your journey.

So, how did the whole idea for the 'Secrets Exposed' books come about?

Well, in 1998, when I was around seventeen, my nan gave me a copy of a book titled *Collective Wisdom*, by Brett Kelly. In it were transcripts of face-to-face interviews with a whole lot of prominent Australian personalities. And it was a fantastic read. Since then I have seen a handful of random 'success story' books, but the challenge I find with most of them is that they are either transcripts of interviews, that never really make complete sense in the printed form, or they are written by writers who paraphrase someone else's story. The result tends to be a diluted message that doesn't really allow you to get a sense of the individual's personality or character.

In around 2001 I read my first *Chicken Soup for the Soul* book and realised that there were dozens and dozens of related titles designed to meet the needs of different people's areas of interest. I thought that was pretty neat.

It wasn't until January 2004 that the 'Secrets Exposed' idea boiled over. I was in my hotel room in Singapore relaxing after six straight days of presenting to hundreds of teenagers. I was reflecting on the ideas that had been shared with them. One of the most important was to seek out those who have already achieved what you want and ask them lots of questions. I was plagued by the thought that only a small percentage would act on that very valuable advice and that most would never take the step due to a lack of confidence, fear of rejection or an inability to contact the people they needed.

That's when it hit me…'What if I could find the people and put together a number of books covering a range of different areas?' I knew it would take a lot of effort, so for the next three days, I sat in my hotel room and developed the basis of an entire system to make it happen.

Based on my experience with other books, I decided that these books had to be non-time specific and be written (not spoken) by the people themselves. This way the answers would be planned and well thought-out, providing richer content and more interesting reading. I also wanted to make sure that there was an even balance between practical 'how to' information and inspirational stories that gave an insight into the highs and lows of people's real journeys. I also wanted to ensure that a percentage of every book sold was donated to a charity relating to the nature of that particular book.

When I arrived home I got into action. However, between working out of a tiny one-bedroom flat and trying to manage two other demanding businesses, my plans were a little slow in the beginning and I had to be resourceful. So I bought a plastic tub and turned the boot of my car into a mobile office! Anytime I could find a spare hour or two, I'd park myself at the gym or a nearby coffee shop and make calls from my mobile phone.

Putting these books together has been both time-consuming and demanding, but it has also been a real privilege for me to have the opportunity to work with each of the people involved in the various books. Thank you, to each of you, for making it possible!

Well, I think you've heard enough from me. Now it's time for you to discover for yourself the wonderful wisdom contained in these pages. I hope that you enjoy the read as much as we've enjoyed putting it together. And who knows, maybe one day we will be reading your story?

Dream Big!

Dale Beaumont
Creator of the 'Secrets Exposed' Series
Sydney, Australia

FOREWORD

Whenever I meet people for the first time, it's almost guaranteed that sometime during the conversation the word 'inspiration' will come up. And while I feel very flattered that people see me in that light, I also see it as a sign of how much in need people are today of positive role models.

What I love most about this book is that its entire focus is on inspiring stories. And what's even better is that these are not celebrities but real women that we can all relate to and take real inspiration from.

The women in this book share their experiences from their hearts and prove to us that we can all do great things. Whether it's starting a business, helping your community, achieving in sport, being a great wife and mother or reaching the heights of a corporate career, they show us that it's all possible and that the only true measure of success is our own.

I owe a lot of my own success to staying positive and surrounding myself with motivated people, which isn't always easy. We can't always ditch the boss or totally escape from a negative relative, but it is possible to take a few minutes of quiet time and let the words in this book come alive so they can be a part of your world.

When I was 16 I travelled to Holland to compete in my first international event. It was there that I had the opportunity to see my sport at its most elite level and witness the best female racer in the world – I knew that very minute I wanted to be just like her. I returned home announcing to family and friends that I was going to become a professional athlete and earn a living from my sport – a decision that some described as 'stupid' and others as 'bold'. Along the way there were many people who inspired me to challenge myself, to defy those that said 'you can't' and to turn my dreams into life-long golden memories.

If you already own this book, keep reading and let these women touch your life – then share it with all the women you know so that we can all become inspiring women in our own lives.

Louise Sauvage OAM
13-time Paralympic medalist
Australian Female Athlete of the Year (1999)
World Sportsperson of the Year with a Disability (2000)
International Female Wheelchair Athlete of the Year (1999, 2000)
Australian Paralympian of the Year (1994, 1996, 1997, 1998)

INTRODUCTION

The title of this book may be 'Inspiring Women', but as you read each chapter you will come to realise that as well as being inspirational, the women in this book share many other qualities that have enabled them to become the 'forces to be reckoned with' that they are today. So, what other aspects of their personalities have led to them becoming the inspirational women that they are?

- *Real* – The women featured in this book share their inner thoughts and the truth about the various aspects of their lives in an extremely candid way. They talk as openly about their achievements as they do about their mistakes, giving us all hope about our own abilities and comfort in being 'only human'.

- *Courageous* – These women have all challenged the norm. Whether it was going against the expectations of their peers, breaking free from a destructive marriage or taking on the challenge of being a mother and having a full-time career – they have all shown us that whatever it is we want to achieve, it can be done.

- *Enterprising* – The women in this book may not all operate their own businesses, but they are all ambitious and enterprising by nature. That doesn't mean they are women trying to live in a man's world. Far from it. They simply believe in the principle that you reap what you sow and they know that happiness comes from being in control of your own decisions rather than at the mercy of someone else's.

- *Have a voice* – Perhaps the most exciting trait these women share is that they are not afraid to take a stand and share from their hearts. At a time when some believe that less of what we say really matters, these women are challenging this notion, each having developed their own vehicle for making a difference and positively impacting everyone they meet.

So while they may not have achieved international fame for wearing the latest red-carpet fashions or their most recent surgical lift, they *have* achieved the sort of fame that is to be envied – they are famous within their own communities for being inspirational, for sharing touching stories that we can all relate to and giving us the strength and motivation to do all of the things in our lives that we never thought we would be able to.

In *Secrets of Inspiring Women Exposed!* we've assembled an amazing group of successful women who are eager to share their experiences and pass on what they've learnt. As for the content, you will see that we have covered a lot of ground: goal setting, communication skills, career advice, maintaining a positive attitude, achieving work/life balance, starting a business, overcoming limiting beliefs, stress management, healthy living, raising children, defining your purpose, increasing productivity, becoming financially secure, and much, much more.

To further assist you in your own endeavours, a number of contributors have also very generously offered valuable gifts to all of our readers. To receive them, all you need to do is visit the website address provided and follow the steps to download the bonus gifts – absolutely *free*.

At the back of the book we have included the contact websites of every contributor. You'll discover that many have their own books or educational materials, which we strongly endorse and encourage you to investigate further.

Finally, remember it's what you do *after you read this book* that is going to determine its real value to you. So, go out there, apply what you've learnt and when you reach a goal – no matter how big or small – let us know so we can share your success story.

ENJOY!

Dale Beaumont and Emma Lyons

Email: info@SecretsExposed.com.au

Rosie Pekar

ROSIE PEKAR

66 The truth is, if you give up then you will never know what you can do. With a bit of persistence even the snail made it to the ark. 99

ROSIE PEKAR

Rosie Pekar was born in Albury, New South Wales, in 1966. As the third child of immigrant Ukrainian parents, she arrived 10 and 13 years after her siblings into a home of domestic violence, fear and loneliness. Although a naturally friendly, curious and adventurous child she felt abandoned and isolated from a young age, and rebelled against her attacker at the age of 14 by running away from home.

As she faced an uncertain life on the streets her only philosophy on life was that it involved suffering. So began her exploratory journey to discover life's meaning. Over the years that followed she married an alcoholic, attempted suicide, and broke-down before she was able to break-through.

At 21 Rosie joined the police force and was exposed to the brutalities, lies and corruption of the criminal world. Eight years later she continued her legal career as a private investigator and security specialist trainer. During this time she also worked as a fitness leader and provided specialist programs to physically and mentally handicapped children and adults.

Today, Rosie is a 'But-kicker' – author, motivator and columnist read by more than 60,000 entrepreneurs globally. She travels regularly, delivering seminars and 'Deliberate Creation' workshops in Australia, New Zealand, Singapore, Thailand, Hong Kong, and the US. Her emergency services role and investigative abilities led her to a KickBut® mind-set that has her thinking on her feet and getting results irrespective of adverse circumstances. These same characteristics transformed her personal life and now serve her well in the global world of business, teaching teams how to create, inspire, serve and lead with passion and a positive perspective over any adversity.

Based on the Gold Coast, Queensland, Rosie is the author of *Time to KickBut®* and has featured regularly in the media in both Australia and the US.

What has been the greatest moment in your life so far and why?

It's hard to choose one great moment out of so many. I've met so many intensely fascinating individuals and celebrities, and have had so many experiences that have deeply touched my heart. However the greatest moment in my life so far would be the passing away of my father. Let me explain…

For the first 14 years of my life, my father had been my worst nightmare, and the next 16 were turbulent at best! Our relationship was based on trouble and violence, so when my mother died 12 years ago, I suddenly felt alone. It was the day after she passed that a stranger, aged in his seventies, came to my home with a letter that he claimed was a message from my now-deceased mother. I read, 'Now is the time for you and your father to grow and love each other'. I scoffed with as much indignity as I could muster, 'That's not from my mum; she knows we hate each other!' Yet some faint glimmer of hope and optimism that the impossible may be possible made me copy that note out and give it to my father, who read it at the time with apparent disinterest.

In January 2005 I was in Indonesia helping with trauma relief operations after the 2004 Boxing Day tsunami when I received a phone call. My father had suffered a heart attack and was not expected to live. At the hearty age of 85, Dad had already beaten the odds and survived many similar incidents. It wasn't an easy decision to leave my position in Banda Aceh and at first I was torn between two loyalties. It felt callous to leave so many desperate and homeless people behind, the clean up of 500 corpses a day had just ended and there was so much work to do in a place that had reportedly lost over 200,000 lives. Despite our unsettled past, my father and I had made peace several years earlier. He had told me that he loved me and asked for forgiveness for all that had transpired between us. As he expressed how proud he was of me, I promised him that I would be with him when it was his time to leave this world. Standing in the extreme heat of Indonesia I heard my father's hoarse voice, 'I'm at the end of my road, Rosie'. I flew home immediately.

> 66 I later discovered that my father's heart attack and the quick transit flights saved my life! 99

I sat by my father's bedside for 24 hours, holding hands with him as he slipped in and out of consciousness. I watched Dad leave as his body finally went into a spasm and let go of its tentative hold on life. His final gift to me was the blessing of life and closure, and we both knew it! In retrospect, my father gave his life to save mine. I got to spend three more weeks absorbing his delighted mischievous chuckle and wildly optimistic and positive outlook on life, which did not abate even in his dying days. He still had so much to teach me about love, gentleness, kindness and forgiveness! Whoever said, 'You can't teach an old dog new tricks' never knew my dad!

Although it was not my happiest moment, it was definitely the greatest and most powerful moment of my life – the total unashamed and unconditional love of my father.

Among his belongings I found the well-worn and tattered message from my mother, no longer a message but an accurate prediction. 'Now is the time, you will both come to love each other…' and I needed no further proof of this man's love.

You believe that your father's heart attack saved your life. Can you explain what you mean?

Amazingly, just four hours after receiving the call that informed me of my father's illness, I was at the military airport in Aceh being transported by Hercules to Medan. I later discovered that my father's heart attack and the quick transit flights saved my life! You see, I'd contracted cholera and without warning, or any sinister signs, it kicked-in embarrassingly at Kuala Lumpur airport. Being in air-conditioned comfort meant that I was able to be quickly hydrated, an unlikely prospect if I had remained in the humidity of Indonesia, where we were drinking six litres a day just to maintain hydration (and for those that don't know, cholera can kill in four to six hours!).

What has been one of the biggest challenges you have had to face in your life and how did you overcome it – how did it shape your life?

The biggest challenge I have had to face, and one that I continually have to overcome, is me! Now, this may sound strange considering that I've had to overcome the fiery and violent nature of burly angry men intent on bashing me with baseball bats, tyre levers and bricks; that I had a contract taken out on my life within my first six months of policing; that I had to prepare myself to jump off a third-floor balcony in order to escape from a man with a shotgun; and that I had to face a knife-wielding man who kept reminding me that he was 'ready to carve me up'. Hmmm…yep, I am definitely my own biggest challenge!

Why? Because of my own mind-set and habitual limiting thoughts. I have met many other people with the same problem or as I like to call it, 'poor-me-itis'. Essentially it's when people blame everything on a specific moment in their life. Unfortunately, we get conditioned to keep on repeating our story – 'poor me I grew up with…' or 'I was diagnosed with…' or 'I was abused by…' The truth is, if you live long enough you'll always have a story to tell, the challenge is to not hinge the rest of your wellbeing on it. That is, don't use it to restrict your personal power for a happy life. It's the thoughts in our heads that make us prisoners to the past and keep us locked into our 'feeling bad' states. Then we wonder why more bad stuff keeps happening to us and lay blame on anything and anyone. Once we understand that it's not 'out there' and that the problem is 'in here' (nasty self-talk) then we are at least on the right track to the root of the problem.

I have met some professional victims alongside career criminals. I call them professional because as I see it they have mastered the art of criticising and condemning while holding themselves aloof. (Yep, guilty as charged, your honour! I especially excelled through my teens and early twenties.) Some will justify the validity of their claims, 'I have every right to feel bad, mad, tired, or whatever' and sadly it becomes their way of being in their life. Not only is this sad for them, it's toxic for all those around them too, and we all know someone like this. I have even watched one die holding onto this attitude.

'Live a life so that when you die, even the undertaker is sad.' Since you can't escape your thoughts I choose to continually challenge myself and believe in more than I dreamed possible. I choose to make my self-talk my friend – not my enemy. Why not make your thoughts something that is exciting and makes you feel good, and in the process attract fabulous results into your life? Makes sense to me!

You call yourself a professional 'but-kicker'. Why is that?

But-kicking is mental empowerment (there's only one 't', so it's not physical!). I help people create positive results by being exceptionally challenging and confrontational to what's not working in their lives. My job in the corporate environment is to create extreme teams and inspire extreme leadership and management. Often this does not come about without resistance or a fight. While some people are willing to change there are always some who want to stay the same, so getting rid of our collective excuses, cop-outs and 'buts' as to why we can't have what we want can be very difficult. That's when they call in a professional to help KickBut®!

Is there a significant quote or saying which you live your life by?

KickBut® – Get rid of the 'Bloody Useless Thoughts' that hold you back!

I have never met anyone who was born with an instruction manual. We are our own teachers and we learn from results in life. Unfortunately, negative experiences often lead to focusing on the negative and this can make us wallow in self-pity and use that most soul-destroying of all words: BUT. For me, B.U.T stands for 'Bloody Useless Thoughts!' You have phenomenal power, literally at your fingertips, so you need to work with the one thing you've always had – your thoughts. Win the battle of the brain and you'll get what you want out of life. As a child I was always told that I was 'bloody useless'. Now it's a positive reframe because no one is saying that anymore, it's just someone else's thoughts that are no longer relevant to me.

You either have the results you want in life or the reasons for not having them, which are not real, just some Bloody Useless Thoughts. Once you have identified the BUTs in your life, the challenge is to replace them with the results you want...accept no cop-outs, no excuses, and no BUTs, that's how to KickBut! Your thoughts, your life, your choice.

Growing up, what or who were some of your early influences in life?

When I was growing up I was an avid reader and had an unquenchable thirst for knowledge in all things esoteric, metaphysical or spiritual. I could not understand my life of turmoil and was desperately seeking an escape or an answer. At the age of nine, I first read a book titled *A Soul's Journey*, which gave me a belief and support system that helped offer solutions to all of my many questions pertaining to life and purpose. Other authors such as Sanaya Roman, Emmet Fox, Florence Scovell Shinn, Norman Vincent Peale, Jane Roberts, Napoleon Hill, Harold Sherman, Wayne Dyer and Gary Zukav all proved invaluable resources, among many others.

What made you decide to get involved in the police force and private investigation?

I had been a volunteer at St George School for Crippled Children in Rockdale, when I saw an advertisement for the police force

66 Not only is this sad for them, it's toxic for all those around them too... 99

and thought 'why not?' It was the solution to my problem of job security and my desire to help people. Six weeks after applying and going through all of the exams and physical fitness tests, I was training at the Goulburn Police Academy, which was the start of my eight-year career as a police officer. After leaving the police force, private investigation seemed like a natural progression. I liked keeping my mind stimulated by the challenges that frauds, thefts and arsons presented, it's the creative linking that is unravelled piece by piece that soon reveals the truth of an incident. In addition, there are laws for evidence that are equally as relevant in life skills. The ability to prove or to disprove in an unbiased manner based on consistency, relevance and sequencing of evidence is a tremendous asset. Often people jump the gun and condemn and judge by what they see or believe to be true, based on very little tangible evidence. As a cop I learnt very quickly that looks and appearances can be very deceptive!

What affect did being a police officer have on your personal life? Was it hard for you to separate yourself from the disturbing things that were going on around you?

Extremely! I was 21 and thrust into a world of hatred and brutality, seeing what other people were capable of doing to each other, observing the lowest of human actions and grossest behaviour and having to report it in detail. I observed human tragedies, witnessed the death and dying of adults and children and was often helpless in the process. I had to face-off with hordes of strangers intent on harming me and calling me every undesirable name in the book and then some! Being the leader and authority in charge in all these events to bring about a resolution, rescue or arrest is quite a daunting task, sometimes even more so at five-foot-two!

At such a young age I didn't have the skills to ensure that these things didn't affect me and I doubt that many young people would. So it was definitely very difficult for me to separate my work from my personal life.

What advice would you give to other women who may be involved in a career that is surrounded by a lot of negativity?

Change careers or refocus on what is working and inspires you. Life is too precious to squander it and waste time on being unhappy, bitter or miserable. For me, the police force had served its purpose in my life and it was no longer necessary for me to stay. And to be honest, I hadn't realised what immense pressure and stress I was under until one year after I left, when a friend said to me, 'Wow Rosie, you're no longer like a cat on a hot tin roof, what's happened?' I now live a life that is full of adventure, fun and purpose without being threatened on a daily basis.

Have you ever had a time in your life where you crashed and lost the will to get back up?

Yes, I wrote about one such personal challenge in *Time to Kick But!*:

'At the age of 28 I had seen one domestic too many. The woman's face was pulverised beyond recognition. Baseball bats do that! She had been dragged by the hair along a bitumen footpath and lost half the skin off her body. I saved her that night, but the odds told me she would return for more. I had seen one distraught spouse too many as I told them of the circumstances of their loved one's death. I had seen one body too many, laying on the roadway in two pieces. How do you comfort the partner sitting nearby? I did my best. I had seen one child too many who had been brutalised and raped and was now required to tell me the sordid details. How do you explain to a child that this brutality is not love, as they are sent back home to their abuser? I had seen one man too many die, despite my valiant efforts to revive him with CPR. His wife held me as I, the policewoman, cried! Driving the ambulance at 40kph, I listened in agony and helplessness as my mother lay dying in the back. All to no avail. Everything seemed to no avail. I did not understand and my faith was sorely tested. I could not understand life's events. What was the point in trying if it did not make any difference?'

> **66 If you cannot connect with someone positively, leave them be... 99**

At the time of these experiences, my marriage had just broken up and I had so many unresolved past issues that I was a cesspool of negativity, sadness and apathy. I'd love to write that I had an instant resolution, but the change for me came about with self-discovery and with time. It's funny how some of us need to hit rock bottom before we work out that we have permission to say, 'Enough, no more! I do not allow this to continue!' We can stop punishing ourselves for perceived misdeeds of the past by no longer remaining in the same environment or allowing others to continue their abuse. We finally work out that by the mere fact that we exist, we are entitled to a happy life, and that we are the ones that give it to ourselves. Once I learnt this, it was no longer necessary for me to be a police officer.

What were some of the most valuable life lessons you learnt during this time?

The power of observation! That everything is about me, a reflection of me. I soon learnt that what was common to every problem I had in my life was *me*. When I was angry I attracted more incidents to make me angry, when I was sad and disheartened I attracted more sadness and became overwhelmed. But when I lightened up and laughed…guess what? I attracted more laughter and happiness. I learnt to become responsible for my 'feeling' states and this was my choice and my power. When I talk at schools I always tell the kids, 'What other people think of you is none of your business'. It keeps their focus on what's real and important, which is their own thoughts and feelings. These thoughts and feelings are creating their world.

What was the turning point that led you on a new direction in life?

Just like anyone else I had several life-changing incidents. I fled home at an early age, ended a dysfunctional marriage, left a secure career with the police force, dealt with the death of my mother and childhood best friend, and faced many life-threatening circumstances. All of these were great learning experiences for expanding, growing and developing a depth of understanding.

My most recent turning point involved a trek in the uninhabited and inhospitable wilderness of Prince Albert Region Park. After walking over 60 kilometres, I suffered extreme heat exhaustion and dehydration (44-plus degree temperatures). With the nearest settlement being over 1,000 kilometres away, sleeping only metres from crocodiles proved to me that my trust in universal laws was complete. It was at this time that I had an out-of-body-experience, which revealed my life experiences with a specific reflection on all the feelings I had toward the people of my past and the emphasis was on how I made other people feel. For me, this has been the greatest turning point in my life and one that has led me in a new direction: find more ways to feel good and less ways to feel bad. This includes all the opportunities that you have to connect with other people – you leave an energetic personalised fingerprint and it's either toxic or beautiful, there's no in-between. If you cannot connect with someone positively, leave them be. They are in their own learning space and it's not necessary to make their 'blah' yours. I know that when you die you will not receive an 'A' critique for having the flattest stomach, the nicest car, the best school for the kids. You may instead re-experience how you made others feel. This keeps my focus on creating win-win situations or the best possible outcome for all involved, irrespective of who they are or what they have done before. It helps me forgive, knowing that it is not about them – it's about how I choose to act as a person. This allows my mind to release turmoil and happily accept every new moment. Most of the time!

In your opinion how does our mind work?

Thoughts create our reality and as we think, we are. Unfortunately, the bulk of our thoughts are habits created or implanted so long ago that we have little conscious directive of what we are actually thinking. So the 60,000 or so thoughts that go through our minds every day are on autocue, otherwise known as reacting. We react to whatever is occurring in the moment or to whatever we are replaying from the past. In doing so, we project this mentality into the future and we get more of the same, which is great if it's what you want. But what if it's not?

There is plenty of mental space to use by challenging our minds to grow beyond our previous limited thinking and beliefs. It's a bit like having a whole planet to live on and just remaining in the one town, yet professing to know what the rest of the world is like. None of us know what we can do or are capable of until we have at least tried. A friend, Shinta Waters, describes people in three categories: we have the pilots and the co-pilots who enjoy directing their destiny, the passengers who are just along for the ride, and the hijackers who are there to screw everyone else's day. It does not take a lot of imagination to work out who is who in life, often it's the result of what thoughts go through their mind.

Why do we sometimes sabotage our own success?

Fear, habit, programmed patterns and RUTs (Repeating Useless Thoughts). Remove that one restrictive word, BUT, from your vocabulary and notice the results! The domain of the mind is phenomenal, although equally daunting is the prospect that there is so much we don't know when it comes to the realms of mind, body and spirit. What we can't identify, we don't rectify and so we often argue extensively to keep the status quo (even when that may be harming or killing us). Socrates uttered immortal instructions thousands of years ago when he said, 'Know thyself', this was passionately followed by many spiritual leaders advising us to 'love ourselves' because what we can accept in ourselves is what we can give to others.

Do you believe that we have complete control over our circumstances?

Yes and no. I have the ability to learn Russian, but will I? No, because I am not interested, although I can if I change my mind and develop that interest. The same principle applies to life. Most of us are not interested in taking control of our own lives, we would rather be consumed by them instead.

There are laws of creation and attraction that countless cultures have documented from over 10,000 years ago, from the Ancient Egyptians and Sumerians to the Buddhists and Hindus. They link the human consciousness to the ability to change vibrating patterns to manifest our desires. In fact, quantum physics is tending to prove that all consciousness at a microscopic level is made of the same 'energy' although it is different in appearance (density) due to the speed rate of vibration of the 'energy'. For example, ice, water and steam are all water molecules, however, the different density makes them appear different to each other. Without knowing better, they would almost appear unrelated. This is the same for the manifestation of our desire, in that we think thoughts are unrelated to events that transpire because of the time delay. So in my opinion, do we have complete control? No. Do we have the *ability* to have complete control? Yes!

What does success mean to you and how do you know you have achieved it?

Having the freedom and passion to pursue unlimited opportunities in creating tools or services for change, growth and prosperity are, for me, my key links – and joy and wellbeing are good indicators of success achieved. The friends, great trips around the world and money are pretty good too!

66 Do we have the ability to have complete control? Yes! 99

One of your favourite phrases is 'do until'. Can you tell us why?

As my friend Graham Alford says, 'Never, ever give up', and he spent years in jail! I say 'do until' because you have the ability to fulfil your dreams. Success often follows on the heels of adversity, however, it's that adversity that stops people in their tracks. What's more, it then introduces a pattern of fear that people stay with rather than venturing into the great unknown. Which, by the way, is where your success lies.

I once had a dream to appear on a popular US talk show, which some people thought (and told me) was silly. Fortunately for me I didn't listen to them and was invited to turn that dream into a reality. The truth is, if you give up then you will never know what you can do. With a bit of persistence even the snail made it to the ark.

tully ©

Having conducted hundreds of radio interviews, what is the most common question asked and how do you answer it?

Everyone always asks about a friend or about a problem that is not theirs! I always ask why? 'Do you not have enough problems of your own that you need more?' This question challenges people to maintain focus on the things they can control – their life, their way of thinking, and their being. The next most popular question is, 'Did you ever shoot anybody?' to which I always reply, 'Not yet!'

What are your five favourite books and why?

- *A Course in Miracles* – The Foundation for Inner Peace
- *Personal Power through Awareness* – Sanaya Roman
- *Conversations with God: Book Three* – Neale Donald Walsch
- *The Power of One* – Bryce Courtney
- *Time to KickBut!* – Rosie Pekar

I regard these as my five favourite books because of their inspiration and empowerment – and the last one because I also wrote it!

Having been exposed to a mix of people from all walks of life, what's your theory on life?

That just like there are many spokes in a wheel all leading to the centre, so too there is no one and only 'right' way to live life (despite many people trying to tell us so!). There are many different personality profiles for amassing wealth, for example Bill Gates' path to monetary success is not the same path as Oprah Winfrey's, Donald Trump's, or Ray Kroc's or Richard Branson's. Each has a distinct character as well as rules for doing what they do. Following our bliss, our natural inclinations and tendencies in alignment with our core personalities, leads us to our wealth. It makes sense then to follow in the footsteps of someone similar to you. The same applies for accruing religious, spiritual, mental, political and personal beliefs. A violet and daisy may both be flowers, although each is decidedly different in being and all make for a spectacular garden. We have such diversity here. I advise people to find what works for them. We are not all at the same age or stage of life. One is not better than another; they are just different and that is the appeal of this planet, contrast and diversity. By knowing what we don't want, we discover what we do!

'Why do you try so hard to blend in, when you were born to stand out?'

 # FREE BONUS GIFT

Rosie Pekar has kindly offered a FREE BONUS GIFT valued at $19.95 to all readers of this book...

The Art Of Powerful Living – Over the last ten years Rosie Pekar has made her mark as the world's best But-Kicker. In this delightful e-book you'll receive inspirational ideas that you'll need to discover the path to taking control of your life. Packed with dozens of tips and notable quotes that will focus your mind, you'll learn the art of powerful living.

Simply visit the private web page below and follow the directions to download direct to your Notebook or PC.

www.SecretsExposed.com.au/inspiring-women

Mia Freedman

MIA FREEDMAN

66 Stop judging yourself against celebrities.
They lie – they pretend that they don't diet, they
pretend they don't exercise and they pretend
they don't have nannies. They pretend they have
perfect lives and it's simply not true. 99

MIA FREEDMAN

Mia Freedman was born in Sydney in 1971. With a working feminist as a mother, Mia was never confused as to whether she would be a stay-at-home or working mother.

After finishing high school, she lived in Italy for a while before returning home to start a communications degree. Admitting to not being a very good student, Mia participated in work experience at *Cleo* magazine. After completing just one year of her degree, she dropped out of university and worked in a variety of part-time jobs while still doing work experience with *Cleo*.

After three or four months, Mia was given the junior role of beauty writer at *Cleo*. She worked her way up to feature writer but decided to go freelance after being passed over for a promotion. When she was 25, Mia was offered an editorship with *Cosmopolitan* magazine, a role she held for eight years. After successfully completing over 100 issues and being awarded the Australian Editor of the Year, Mia moved up to become editor-in-chief of *Cosmo, Cleo* and *Dolly*.

In 2006 Mia broadened her media career by becoming creative service director at Channel Nine and has recently helped launch *The Catch-Up* – a smart and entertaining daytime television show for women.

Mia enjoys writing, running, and the sound of her own voice. Her favourite way to spend time is with her family, including her husband and two kids, Luca and Coco.

When you first started working at *Cleo*, was it your ambition to become editor or was it a goal that evolved over time?

I started at *Cleo* doing unpaid work experience and decided I wanted to be editor by the time I was 25 years old. It was a goal that I clung to with both hands, but for a while it started to look like it wasn't going to happen. I was passed over for promotion a couple of times and I was devastated by the idea that my dream might not come true so I left, got a bit disillusioned, and thought I might start doing something different. I eventually let go of that idea and soon after I was offered the job of editing *Cosmo*. Go figure.

You were offered the job of *Cosmo* editor at a young age. Was it difficult managing and working with people who were sometimes twice your age?

I didn't find it difficult because I was an overconfident person. When I started at *Cosmo* everyone was older than me and I certainly made some mistakes with my management style. I was also very impatient to have a new team because I didn't want a team that was constantly telling me 'But we've always done it THIS way…' You want to have people who are loyal to you and are concentrating on your vision (instead of concentrating on making a comparative analysis). So it was important to build *my* team even though it took a few years. It was even more important to have a team of people who really wanted to be there. I may have started off with staff who were older than me, but eventually I ended up with a younger team. In some ways they were just as difficult to manage because often they lived highly dramatic lives, as twenty-somethings do…break-ups, partying…always a drama.

Early in your career, what were a few of the most important lessons that you learnt?

I learnt that I was very overconfident. The older I got, the more I found I didn't know. It's a lesson that I'm still learning.

> 66 I am amazed how much I have enjoyed training other people and working with them. 99

Managing staff is something that you never really learn. As an editor you usually go down the path of being a journalist first. Journalists are very good with words but that may not mean they are very good with people. Managing and nurturing staff is something that I learnt through trial and error, and fortunately I really loved it. There are some incredible editors who are terrible at managing staff and they end up with an unhappy team. I am amazed how much I have enjoyed training other people and working with them. Seven of my staff from *Cosmo* have gone on to become editors of other national magazines. I'm not going to take credit for the jobs they got, but to be able to say I was involved is a great feeling.

Also, never lose sight of your market and who they are. I think a lot of people forget who they are producing their magazine (or product or service) for and they start doing it to impress their friends or peers. That's a classic mistake.

What would you say to people that may think they are too proud to work for free?

Good Luck! I was part of Generation X and therefore willing to do whatever it took to get into the magazine industry. I have since noticed that Gen Y-ers can be hugely impatient and aggressively ambitious. I have both those qualities so I can relate. But if you're not willing to do the menial tasks first, you may not get a chance to get your foot in the door, let alone be promoted. I understand they all have degrees, which I didn't have at that stage, but whether it's work experience, working for free or getting someone's coffee, if it gets you in the door then that's what you need to do. In fact, you'd be crazy not to do whatever it takes!

With special body love guest editor Sara-Marie

COSMO ITAN

soul mate or just
a date? YOU + HIM tarot card
LOVE FORECAST

**sex up
YOUR LOOK**
BEAUTY MOVES SO HOT YOU'LL
MELT HIS PADDLE POP

**MILLIONAIRE?
WHO CARES!**
219 NEW-TREND-BUYS
FROM $5.95!!

'I HAD SEX WITH
**251 MEN IN
10 HOURS"**

**"I'm not anorexic"
SKINNY GIRLS**
BITE BACK

Emotional Abuse
A shocking report
you MUST read

BONUS
FLIP-OVER
COVER:
Britney
+ budget
fashion
spesh

**4 STEPS
TO ALL-SIZE
BODY
CONFIDENCE**
love
Sara-Marie

YOUR BOYF'S SECRET LIFE Do you REALLY want to know?

Mia's 'risk taking' cover while editor of *Cosmopolitan*.

When you began your role as editor, you started taking a lot of risks. What are some of the major risks you took and why were you willing to take them?

There was one major risk I took (to the horror of my boss) and that was to put bigger girls on the pages of *Cosmo*. I had grown up with women's magazines and I had seen the damage they could do in terms of unrealistic body images and diets, which ultimately made women feel bad about themselves. I knew, as a reader, when I flicked through the pages and saw all of these skinny models I felt bad about myself. But I knew that doing something different could be bad for the brand and I knew it would be taking a huge gamble. The moment I put a size 16 model in a fashion shoot, it became a talking point in the industry. Everybody was horrified! The photographer didn't want to be credited and no one wanted to send clothes for the shoot. Even though my boss wasn't thrilled about the idea, she had the confidence in me to say, 'Let's try it'. The readers loved it! So in the end it turned out to be a great doorway for a huge marketing push and it influenced our 'Body Love' campaign. All of a sudden the magazine was showing women of all sizes. Circulation and readership went through the roof, as did advertising. It was the start of a real growth phase for *Cosmo* – literally!

Some critics claim that all beauty magazines promote low self-esteem. What is your opinion?

This was something I tried to tackle when I first started in magazines. I think there can be some truth in the accusation but I also believe that magazines are a great way to educate. In the seventies, magazines used to portray golden-brown models baking in the sun and smoking cigarettes. These days magazines can deliver powerful messages such as smoking is bad for your health, the sun can cause skin cancer, and practise safe sex. It's about balance. Today I feel disappointed when I look in a magazine and see only one type of skinny girl. But all I could do was try to make a difference in the magazines I had control over.

Did you feel that your personality began to change with the added responsibility and the need to make strong decisions on a daily basis?

I sometimes find it odd that I'm more assertive in my work life than in my personal life. Having said that, I'm not confrontational. I'll work around an issue, I never raise my voice at work and never have. I'm very nurturing to my staff and I always maintain great working relationships with all my colleagues. I'm no *Devil Wears Prada*! Although at the end of my time in magazines, I certainly became less tolerant and less patient with people who weren't doing their jobs properly. I have high standards but I'm fair. Managing a team of staff is like being one of those people who spin plates on sticks – just when you think they're all spinning, one goes wobbly and you have to attend to it. It's very rare that all the plates are spinning perfectly at the same time. The biggest change for me was when I gave birth to my first child. It really changed me as a person. I had more perspective and I was more efficient. I like to think I got better at my job as I got older – I certainly got more efficient at doing it. Having kids changes you in every way.

How did becoming a mother influence your work?

I had only been at *Cosmo* for a little while when I fell pregnant with my son (I was about 25 years old). When I told my boss, she said I would be a better editor when I was a mother. And she was right. Being a mother keeps me grounded, especially in an industry that's based on superficiality.

Initially, I never wrote about being a mother when I was at *Cosmo*. That was one of the reasons I knew it was time to move on. Being a mother has become more and more of who I am and influences everything I think and do. That's where writing my newspaper column and bits for other magazines with older audiences have been so great for me. I really needed that creative outlet to talk about issues I think so many mothers face. I love the ability to communicate with other women and show that I am just like everyone else – I do sometimes feed my children tuna from a can and we do have cereal for dinner occasionally. My life is not perfect and I am not any kind of superwoman. I know what it feels like to sit at home and think 'everyone has it together except me' when really they don't at all. Trust me, women

> **66** The biggest change for me was when I gave birth to my first child. **99**

who appear to be perfect never are. We all drop the balls when we're juggling, no matter how much money and fame and support we have. So I try to be as honest as I can. I think if there was more honesty from women who are in the public eye then women everywhere would feel so much better about themselves.

Did you find that having children slowed down your productivity in your career?

After I had my second child, I realised that for about a year after the birth of each of my children I lost my ambition. It's lovely! I mean I just dived into my babies and that's all I cared about. Although I was still involved in work, I took maternity leave and focused everything on my children. Then I started to get itchy feet. Or maybe an itchy brain. I try to strike the right balance and sometimes I get it right and sometimes I get it wrong. It's strange, when I'm at home with my baby I can't ever imagine loving work again, but when I'm back at work I can't imagine being at home full-time again. Being a Libra, I'm always looking for the balance between the two and often I don't find it! But I keep looking because they're both important to me. In terms of productivity, I think mothers are the most efficient people in the world because they have to be. You have no time to sit at your desk and cruise the internet because you want to get out of there and get home to the kids.

What advice would you give to other parents that are trying to juggle work and family?

It's an ongoing struggle for everybody. I certainly won't say I have the answer. You just have to keep trying and be kind to yourself. Find friends in the same boat and support each other. When things feel bleak, reassure each other that no, you're not crap mothers and you're not crap at your job. I think the trick is not beating yourself up over it. And keep reassessing. If it doesn't feel right and if guilt or exhaustion is crippling you, it might be time to make a change.

What are your top tips for women who need to increase their self-esteem and body image?

Stop judging yourself against celebrities. They lie – they pretend that they don't diet, they pretend they don't exercise and they pretend they don't have nannies. They pretend they have perfect lives and it's simply not true. Don't judge yourself by those standards. Go talk to your friends, or your mother, or go to the beach and look at the bodies of real women, rather than reading an interview with Gwyneth Paltrow. We all compare ourselves to other people and I think we do it too much. Instead of looking at what is lacking in our lives, we should look at what gifts we have already.

What are your top fashion tips for everyday women?

Two tips to remember about fashion:

1. It's not brain surgery or rocket science! So have fun with it. At the end of the day it's just clothes, so don't get caught up with labels or what celebrities are wearing.

2. Seek the counsel of men (yes, you heard me correctly). Find out what the men in your life think about what you wear. I don't mean that men should dress you, but they do have an innate ability to cut through all of the distractions and get straight to the point. For example, 'Why are you wearing a pirate shirt?' or 'Why are you wearing a dress over your jeans?' Answers like, 'Well, Cameron Diaz was wearing it!' or 'It's Gucci', have no relevance to men. Give them the space to be honest and then make your decision based on what you feel like wearing today.

Is there any similarity between you and the lead character from *The Devil Wears Prada*?

God, I loved that movie! I think what differs from myself and that character is that I have always been nurturing as a boss, and every personal assistant I have had has gone on to do amazing things because

> **There were a few watershed moments where I knew it was time to leave...**

I've supported and promoted them. I'm always very close with all my staff. There are things that I do identify with in that role though. You do become a bit ivory tower and start to think, 'Why is it so hard to get this done?' And the reason you lose touch with that is because you don't actually do some things anymore and you may not be aware of the process. What a great film though. There are a lot of books and movies written about the magazine industry, so we hear it all and read it all but there was a lot of truth to this particular film.

What mistakes did you make and what did you learn from them?

Someone once told me, 'You learn by commission not omission'. That is, you learn by what you do, not by what you're too scared to do. I think it's very healthy to make mistakes and I was fortunate to have a boss who was willing to let me make them. When I first started at *Cosmo* I made plenty of mistakes and my boss was smart enough to give me just enough rope to learn, but not enough to hang myself or damage the magazine irreparably. For example, one of the first things I did at *Cosmo* (and this is a classic case of editing for yourself and not your readers) was to decide that there were too many sex and relationship articles. I decided to get rid of all of them, which we did – and then we watched circulation go down the toilet. Lesson learnt (and very quickly)! Just because I had moved into a new phase of my life (I was almost a mother) and had moved away from those types of stories, there were still plenty of 18 year olds who wanted to read them. This was a brand that had been around for 40 years and who was I to come in and say that the branding was all wrong? I was ignorant to think that I was going to do better when the branding was already working. After an international *Cosmo* conference, the realisation suddenly dawned on me – I had been given a gift to work with such a strong brand. I could work within the brand and change things around, but really, the strength of the brand was my biggest asset.

What made you decide to leave your job as *Cosmo* editor?

There were a few watershed moments where I knew it was time to leave *Cosmo*. I was there for about 100 issues and some really interesting times in my life. But I needed a new challenge. I was a mother and I felt that my life interests were changing. I think as you get older everyone gets a bit more conservative and I realised that *Cosmo* needed a breath of fresh air. I didn't want to be the face of the magazine anymore, or to carry the banner for sealed sections or have to defend the oral sex articles. As editor-in-chief of *Cosmo*, *Cleo* and *Dolly* – a role I took on after editing *Cosmo* – I enjoyed teaching editors and nurturing them, guiding the magazine, and taking a big picture view. I did this for a year or two before I grew tired of nurturing other people's creativity. I wanted to own something and be more hands on.

Can you describe how your career has progressed in recent years and where you are right now?

After my daughter was born I went on maternity leave. I took a good six months off this time, unlike with my first baby when I didn't mentally have that break and returned to work pretty quickly. It was during those first months after my daughter was born that I decided that I didn't really want to go back. Funnily enough, at about the same time I received a call from Eddie McGuire. I had met him a few times over the years, and having just been appointed as CEO of the Nine Network, he offered me a job. Basically, he was tired of sitting in a boardroom with 20 men trying to work out what women wanted to watch on television. It seemed like a great opportunity, so I accepted. ACP didn't want to lose me but they knew I needed a new challenge so I agreed to stay on as a consultant for their magazines. Initially I completely underestimated the challenge of shifting careers from magazines to television, especially after being at home for six months. It took me a couple of months to find my feet, but now I'm just about to launch a new show and it's incredibly exciting. I feel like my entire career has been leading up to this point.

Tell us about the new show you're going to launch.

It's a daytime television show for women, which is going to be smart, fun and entertaining. I've always enjoyed daytime television because it's women's television. And the audience is different now. It's not just retirees anymore, there are loads of women in their twenties, thirties and forties at home –studying, working from home, working part-time, or looking after kids and babies. I've been there so I know the headspace of the audience intimately.

What I like about my job is that it allows for instant gratification and appeals to my short concentration span. With faster news cycles (as a result of the internet), working on a monthly magazine became a challenge for me because I wanted to do things now. As the show is going to be a one-hour live telecast, five days a week, there is a huge opportunity to do things immediately.

What have been some of the major turning points in your career and what have you learnt from them?

- One of my unhappiest times was when I was in my early twenties. I was holding onto the dream of being the editor of *Cleo* so tightly that I was passed over for promotion. It was only when I let go of that dream that other opportunities came to me. I don't think you can be too narrow in your focus. You need to have an open mind and understand that perhaps the way to get to B is not from A.

- When is it time to leave? When I decided to leave *Cosmo* I realised that I had reached a point where I was about to overstay my welcome. I realised creatively that it was time to move on. I simply didn't want to be a 40-year-old woman writing for *Cosmo* and pretending to be single. It wasn't to say I couldn't have done that, but you need to be true to your passions.

- After having children, a question that I was suddenly confronted with was could I ever be a stay-at-home mum? My answer was ultimately, 'no'. I love my children and my family more than anything in the world but it doesn't fulfil me 100 per cent as a person. I couldn't give my family up but I couldn't give my job up either. I need them both. Sometimes I still feel guilty about this, but it's the truth.

- A few years ago I was offered an editorship in America. It would have been an awesome job. My son was about five years old at the time and I spoke to my husband about it and he was very supportive. It would have been the most amazing thing for my career, but I realised I didn't want to go. I didn't want to live in New York. I mean, it would have put me on an international level and in a wonderful place in my career, but to me the sacrifices to my family and lifestyle were not worth it. I don't regret it for a second. My family is ultimately way more important and I would never want to sacrifice having time with them and watching them grow up in Australia.

Were there any times that you wanted to give up? What got you through?

There have been a number of times when I have thought, 'What do I want to do next?' and 'Do I really want to be doing this?' You just have to wait to see if the feeling goes away. Sometimes it does, and you realise you're just having a bad week. I always just sit with it and not panic. If the feeling doesn't go away, you think, 'Maybe I need to reassess'. Someone once gave me a great piece of advice for making decisions and this was when I was first deciding on whether to take the job at *Cosmo*. I had just left *Cleo* and had gone freelance. This person said, 'If you're torn between ending a relationship or moving house or taking a job offer, imagine that you are definitely doing it. For example, you're taking the job. Think about it for a day and see

> 66 I feel like my entire career has been leading up to this point. 99

how you feel. Then the next day, think that you're definitely not going to take it. Then you work out what you feel. Are you excited? Are you disappointed?' It's a really great way to cut to the heart of it and see what you really want to do. I have used this a number of times when I have been at crossroads in my life.

Is there a significant quote or saying which you live your life by?

'Be yourself, everyone else is taken.'

'No-one can make you feel inferior without your permission.'

What do you believe are the main problems and issues facing young women today?

I think it's balance. You can have children and still have a career but at what level and what cost? The key is finding the balance which means flexible work practices, and quality affordable childcare. With Generation Y entering the workforce this balance is perhaps more achievable. This generation is not interested in having it all, they just want balance in their life. Generation X nearly killed themselves trying to have it all and a lot of them were very unhappy or disappointed at the end of it. There needs to be a balance, whether it's travelling, working or having kids.

Did being a high-powered businessperson affect your relationship at home?

My husband and I were already together before I became an editor. Fortunately for me he has never been threatened by my career. We're each other's biggest support and greatest cheerleaders. He runs his own successful company, and so my success is the family's success, and his success is the family's success too. I guess the only challenge I have had to deal with was coming home after a frustrating day at work and forgetting that my family were not my employees. I had to stop and say to myself, 'This is your family, so stop being the alpha-girl'. It's not just about bringing home the emails, it's also about bringing home the attitude. When you are trying to achieve things at work, you do get tough with people and it's important to take a moment in the car on your way home to try to leave all of that behind you. It's the same when you go to work. Leave your family issues at home, put on your suit mentally and get to work.

What has been the greatest moment in your life so far and why?

Without a doubt, it is meeting my husband and giving birth to my children. I have had numerous career achievements, including Editor of the Year, but none ever came close to those moments and nothing ever will. Those three moments are seared into my heart and my mind as if they happened this morning.

Terry Hawkins

TERRY HAWKINS

" I think there are no greater travesties on Earth than to not fulfil your purpose or to let fear paralyse you. I have been driven my entire adult life to support others in becoming the best they can be. "

TERRY HAWKINS

Terry Hawkins was born in Brisbane in 1961 and is one of six children. Her childhood had none of the trappings of wealth, and the family finances took a turn for the worse when her father passed away when Terry was only 15 years old.

After leaving school, Terry went to college for a short time before working in a variety of jobs, none of which promised to be a long-term career. Eventually she landed a job as a salesperson with a retail clothing company. Determined to make a go of it, Terry treated customers like old friends. It was a philosophy that worked and skyrocketed Terry's sales, boosting her up the corporate ladder. Her infectious enthusiasm transformed unmotivated staff into eager sales team members and she was soon the training coordinator. Terry set out to revolutionise training practices and quickly developed a reputation for excellent staff training in retail circles. She held state and national training roles with major companies until she embarked on a journey to head up her own training company, People In Progress, in 1988.

Over the past 18 years, Terry has built a reputation for heading up one of the most innovative, dynamic and successful training companies in Australia. She is also one of the most highly sought-after female speakers in Australia and New Zealand and has just written her first book, *There Are Only Two Times in Life, Now and Too late!*

Terry lives on the Northern Beaches of New South Wales with her two beautiful sons, Harison and Jackson. When she is not travelling the globe on speaking engagements, her other true passion is developing teenagers in the Pitman/Stickman theory.

Your father passed away when you were only 15 years old. How did this event impact your life?

It was a very confusing and challenging time, not just for me but for my entire family. My mother went back to work as she didn't want to live on benefits from the government, so she relied on me a great deal to help her raise my younger brother and sister and look after the household duties. The greatest impact for me was to watch my mother work so hard. She was a night shift nursing sister for a major hospital and she would walk two kilometres to the train station for a one-hour trip, work all night and then take the same long journey home. When my father died, we had very little money, and we didn't own our own home. My mother secured a housing commission home for us to live in and provided us with a roof over our heads and food on our table every night. She kept it all together for us and at the same time gave me an example of what it meant to work hard.

One of the groups I now do volunteer work with is Carers NSW in their Young Careers Project, having been on the other end when I was younger. I tell these amazing kids that as much as it may seem tough at the time, it is in these tough times that we learn the greatest lessons for our future. We are being prepared and I wouldn't change my past for anything. It was hard at the time and I used to think how unfair it was that I didn't have the easy life that my friends had. I am so grateful now for the life I was given because I know emphatically that I would not be the person I am today without those early experiences. I have a very strong family and work ethic and I am grateful for having fabulous boys and a job that I love. I know that no matter what, I will be able to provide for my boys because I would be willing to do anything for them, just as my mother did for us.

One of your first full-time jobs was in sales. What lessons did you learn during that time?

My first sales job was with a national jeanswear company, and I quickly learnt that not many companies train their new staff to sell well. I was

66 It's a concept that I grew over many years and it has evolved... 99

completely useless when I first started. In fact, I was so useless they wanted to sack me after two weeks! I quickly realised that survival meant I had to work out how to get customers to buy from me. I discovered that if I made people laugh and have a good time they stayed in the store. And the longer they stayed in the store, the more they bought! I started winning some sales competitions and moving up through the ranks. The greatest lesson I learnt was to give people a good time and to make the experience enjoyable and fun. We need to laugh more in business and in life. If you get your customers having fun and enjoying themselves they'll keep coming back for more.

How did you fall into becoming a global business trainer?

The global part happened many years after I started as a trainer. When I look back on my early history, training seemed to be a common thread. Before I started college, I had a job with the YMCA which was extremely varied. I taught gymnastics to primary school kids and fitness to adults. I also worked with Down Syndrome kids teaching physical awareness, and ran holiday programs for latchkey day care kids. When I dropped out of college I had a short stint selling photocopy paper and was then asked to train the telephone sales team. So I suppose training was always there, I just never saw the common thread until I looked back. My first 'real' training role came about when the state trainer for the jeanswear company wanted to be the receptionist! I ambitiously applied for the job because at the time I really didn't know what it involved. After getting the role however, I just relished in it. Seven years later I started my training company, People In Progress, which has given me the opportunity to train and speak all over Australia and the world.

What steps did you take to get to where you are now?

I never really planned to be where I am today and I am ever so grateful for the life I have. I think the factor that has contributed to my success the most is that I have never had money as my primary motivator. My passion for wanting to help people be their best has always been the 'fire in my belly'. I think there are no greater travesties on Earth than to not fulfil your purpose or to let fear paralyse you. I have been driven my entire adult life to support others in becoming the best they can be.

Much of your work revolves around the quirky 'Pitman/Stickman' concept. Can you please explain it to us?

The 'Pitman/Stickman' concept is actually a 90-minute segment out of one of our three-day sales training programs. It's a concept that I grew over many years and it has evolved (and still evolves) into what it is today. Whenever I trained salespeople, managers or administrative people, regardless of the industry or position, there was a common thread – the people who got the results acted and spoke in a different way to the ones who didn't. Those differences became Pitman and Stickman. It's hard to do these wonderful characters justice in such a short space but the quickest way to describe them is to say that these two amazing characters live inside our heads. We have the villain Pitman, who represents our negative state, and we also have our superhero Stickman, who creates our positive state. These two characters create the moment-by-moment perceptions of events and situations that occur daily in our lives.

Pitman – is the villain who lives in the 'The Pit of Misery®'. The Pit is the place we go when we don't think we have any power. It's where we blame everyone and everything for how we're feeling or where we're at in our lives. It's the place we go to when life seems miserable and lonely; when we feel pitiful, when everyone is against us and when no one understands us. When we're in the Pit, we tend to create a powerful suction valve that starts draining the energy and life out of anyone who may project a positive and optimistic view of the world.

Stickman – is the superhero who represents the part of us that is powerful, confident, loved, self-assured and successful. The great thing about Stickman is that we control him just as we control Pitman. When we are in a Stickman state we tend to deal with life a lot better and create far more positive outcomes. Being in a Stickman state actually changes the biological and physiological responses in our bodies. It has been scientifically proven that changing the way we think and act changes the way our bodies respond!

tully ©

You believe that language is very influential in shaping people's attitudes. We take it you're not referring to English, French or Japanese?

You are so right! But it can seem foreign if we are not used to paying attention to our language. When I use the term 'language' I am talking about our internal and external dialogues – the things we say out loud or inside our heads. Often we are not aware of the damaging effect our words can have. We say incredibly negative things to ourselves and others, and our unconscious mind picks up on all of this and believes everything we say.

As I mentioned, Stickman is like our own internal superhero. He only ever speaks to us in a language that improves a situation or the people around him. He's not about blame, but strong on responsibility. When we are in a Stickman state we are completely aware of how we communicate with ourselves and with those around us. We pay strict attention to our internal dialogue. We speak in terms of where we want to end up as opposed to where we are now. Our language spearheads our behaviour.

Why are the words we say to ourselves so powerful?

Whatever we say to ourselves, our unconscious mind believes. So when we say 'I can't do this' or 'I'm no good at something' our unconscious mind believes us. Most of us are completely unaware of the language that we use, therefore we create negative outcomes.

For example, statistics show that on average 75 per cent of the communication in a relationship is negative and only 25 per cent is positive. I think this is because we get into the habit of speaking in a negative manner. After a while we stop paying attention to what we say to those we love, and how we say it. I think we become very conditioned to negative language and stop noticing the damage it causes. Years later we wonder why we don't love each other anymore. Test it for yourself. Ask someone how he or she is. Chances are they will reply with, 'Not bad', 'Getting there', 'I've been better' or something similar.

66 We speak in terms of where we want to end up as opposed to where we are now. 99

Can you list for us some of the words or sentences common to Pitman and Stickman?

The important thing to pay attention to is the pattern of language that we use. A lot of us are not even aware of the negative phrases we use on a constant basis. Some of the Pitman words or sentences we use include:

- The kids are driving me crazy!
- You never help!
- This traffic is ridiculous.
- I'll never make my targets.
- I can't cope with all of this.
- What is wrong with people these days?
- Did you see how rude that person was?
- I'm just so tired!
- Everybody is picking on me.
- Nothing good happens to me.
- I can't do that…
- That won't work!

The Stickman words and sentences that we should be using more include:

- I am doing…
- My kids are just being kids. I'll take a break.
- I'll ask for help if I need it.
- I'll do whatever I can to achieve my targets.
- I appreciate my job.
- Life can be challenging…
- Let's give it a go!
- I'll do my best…
- I am being patient.
- I have everything I need…
- If I'm not satisfied I will do whatever it takes to achieve my goals.
- Maybe that person is tired and that's why they're being a bit cranky.

If you find yourself in a Pitman state, how do you snap out of it?

When you are in a Pitman state, the easiest thing to do is to pretend to be positive through your behaviour, feelings and thoughts. The great thing about the unconscious mind is it doesn't know the difference between fact and fiction. It can't tell when we're faking it. That's why I love the term 'Fake it 'til you make it'. It's quite an easy concept and I think that's why people love Stickman and Pitman.

I was recently interviewed for *The Australian* newspaper and the interviewer asked me, 'If you were to tell someone how to feel motivated, what would you say?'

'There lies the problem!' I replied. 'I aim to run three kilometres most days. Do you think I wake up every day going yippy, yippy, joy, joy! I'm going for a three-kilometre run! No way, especially on those really cold days when Pitman is at the window saying, 'It's cold out here. Stay in bed. You deserve it.' People think that they have to *feel* motivated to *do* motivational things', I continued. 'We think we need the feeling in order to do the behaviour, but we don't. As long as we are clear about the positive outcomes we want, articulate those outcomes using language in a powerful, action-based way and then *do* the behaviours to achieve those outcomes, we will get the result we want, regardless of how we *feel!* So for now, just think about what it is that you *do* that creates negativity in your life, focus on the positive behaviour and then just *do* it!'

If someone believes that they don't have the power, what can you do for them?

First, it's important to identify whether that person really wants to get out of their 'Pit' or not. I know it may seem that everybody would want to be outside the Pit, but for some people it's safer and more comfortable for them to stay in it. Regular visitors to the Pit can actually get a lot of attention and sympathy and this is the main reason they stay there. However, an important point to note here is that the only person that

> 66 She told us how she had stained the pages with tears as she read each line. 99

can get me out of my Pit is me, and the only person that can get you out of your Pit is you. It can be quite easy to be seduced into the game of rescuer and victim because both of these roles live in the Pit. People need to understand that a rescuer needs a victim and a victim needs a rescuer. It's like a continuous dance that they do together. Unconsciously, a rescuer does not want the victim to get better because they would be out of a job! So often we wait for someone else or something else to come along and save us. 'When I get a better job, more money, better education, more time, more sleep, a new partner, then I will feel better.' The great thing about Stickman is you don't have to believe it to do it. You just have to want it bad enough and be willing to do what is required.

Do you have any interesting stories about how your two sons apply your lessons to their lives?

Jackson and Harison refer to Stickman and Pitman all the time! I just love how they relate to the different states they go into. We are not allowed to say 'I can't' in our house because the moment you say 'I can't' the brain supports you. We replaced it with 'I am'. I chuckle when I hear the boys looking for something and then I hear this little voice saying 'I *am* finding my socks, I *am* finding my socks'. It truly is amazing to see children as young as them recognising when they are in a Pit state and using Stickman to change it.

Can you share a couple of notable success stories of people that you have helped over the years?

I cannot begin to tell you how fortunate I feel to have heard the most amazing stories from people who have turned their lives around. There was the mother who chose to climb out of her Pit after years of grieving the death of her son, and there are countless stories of wonderful men who have spoken to me after a presentation with tears in their eyes, acknowledging that they are the Pitman in their families.

I do remember a very simple, yet profoundly wonderful story of a woman who was in one of our three-day programs. I had set an exercise for self-esteem and had asked the group to write out ten traits they liked most about themselves. They were allowed to ask their partner if they found it hard to fill the list. She shared her story with the group the next day.

'When I asked my husband to tell me a few traits he liked about me, he told me to not be silly and just laughed at my request. After 25 years of marriage my husband couldn't even say a couple of things that he liked about me. I went to bed that night with an ache in my heart. When I got up the next morning, after my husband had left for work, I walked into the kitchen and found a couple of sheets of paper on the table – listed on those pages were the reasons why my husband loved me.'

She told us how she had stained the pages with tears as she read each line. She was still having a little cry as she shared her story with us and I don't think there was a dry eye in the room. 'I feel like I've fallen in love with him all over again!' she beamed. Sometimes it's not always the big stories that blow me away. It's just the simple, everyday actions and choices that people make to create a better life for themselves and those they love.

Why do you advise people of all ages to write love letters?

I think writing a letter filled with all the reasons why you love someone is the greatest gift you can give. First, it takes effort and I think in so many relationships we stop making the effort. You can ask any woman why she loves flowers and apart from the fact that they're beautiful to look at and smell, she will tell you, 'It isn't the flowers, it's the fact that he made the effort'. I was speaking to a son (about 30 years old) who had never heard his father say to him 'I love you son!' That just blows my mind. I suggested that he write his father a love letter and by the look on his face you would have thought I had just asked him to swallow 54 venomous spiders! You could tell just the thought of it scared the hell out of him. 'I don't do things like that' was his reply! Unfortunately someone has to go first. If we're going to break the pattern of behaviour that may have gone on for centuries, generation after generation, someone must go first. Just maybe, if he had written a love letter to his dad, he may have opened the door ever so slightly for his father to respond in a similar manner. Sometimes we are the teacher and sometimes we are the pupil. I have never known anyone who has received a love letter that wished they hadn't. We save them forever and revisit them when our heart needs a massage of love. The biggest reason we don't write is that we worry what the other person might think! There are only two times in life, now and too late. So start writing.

You have been a global trainer for over 25 years. What inspires you to keep doing what you do?

There is a wonderful saying, *'We see so far because we stand on the shoulders of giants'*. I have the wonderful opportunity every day to associate with people who want to build, improve, or change their lives for the better and I can't help but be inspired by this. I absolutely love what I do and for the entire 25 years I have loved it. Have I had tough days? Absolutely, and there are times when I find it incredibly challenging. But it only takes one person to say that I'm helping them make different choices to live their life in a more empowered, passionate and positive way and I am back in there doing it again! We all thrive off each other on this Earth and my audiences give me so much to be grateful for. I am extremely lucky.

Was it especially hard to go through your divorce given the work you do and how much people look up to you?

That's an interesting question and I think a lot of the time people are judged on whether their relationships work or not. I think the great thing about the work that I do is that I was forced to face my own truth. I don't just talk this stuff, I truly live it.

I think anybody going through a divorce would find it incredibly difficult regardless of the work that they do. It was probably the most difficult thing I have ever experienced and more so because of my beautiful boys. I don't see people as failing because they get divorced – if anything they have acted on their truth. The part that frustrates me the most is how unwilling some people are to do whatever it takes to make their relationship work. A relationship is two-sided and it may sound ironic, but I have worked out how to have the best relationship you could ever want, with anyone! It involves one sentence and it can apply to any type of relationship – parents, lovers, customers and friends. It takes two to make it work though and both parties must commit to doing it. It is this: find out what the other person wants and just give it to them. If couples lived by that rule and were focused on doing whatever they could to make their partner happy then we would have a lower divorce rate. But like I said, it takes two.

What is the most important thing you have learnt about being a mother, wife, leader and businesswoman?

The greatest attributes you can have for all of those roles are a healthy self-esteem and a good sense of self-worth. For many years I had a low self-esteem and when you have a low self-esteem you make dumb choices! I believe you should do whatever you can to build your self-esteem – hang around people who help build a better you, read books that teach you the same, look after your body, and be kind to yourself and others. You will see a completely different world when you can appreciate yourself and others.

> 66 ...find out what the other person wants and just give it to them. 99

From your experience, what advice would you give to other women that are experiencing major difficulties in their relationships?

The only way out is through! I love that saying because there are no easy paths. I think trust your intuition, then do everything in your power to save your relationship. It is easy to walk away too soon because so many of us are not willing to walk through the pain of finding our way back to each other. And if you do break up, then just remember that the pain in your heart, that endless well of tears and that insurmountable feeling of guilt will subside and be replaced with an inner strength and a knowingness that you will be okay.

The greatest advice I can give anyone who has just separated is to avoid going into another relationship too soon. It is so important to learn how to be single, to learn how to be on your own, and to learn how to enjoy your own company. Learning to be alone was one of the hardest paths I have ever walked but it was the most empowering. I was able to see the patterns that I had created in all of my past relationships and that wouldn't have happened if I had gone straight into another one. Many people think that they are not whole because they don't have a partner, but I think you need to be personally whole before you can find the right partner. It's a hard concept for a lot of us to grasp but I truly wish more people would give it a try.

Is there a significant quote or saying which you live your life by?

Yes, and I named my first book after it: *'There are only two times in life – now and too late!'* I love it because it's true. The only time we have is this moment, right now. The past is gone, even the last two minutes are over and the future hasn't even happened yet so the only power we truly have is in this moment, right here, right now. So give this moment your best.

What do you think holds people back from achieving their goals?

Two things:

1. *Worrying too much about what other people will think of us* – we tend to make decisions that make us look good and we fear putting ourselves in a vulnerable position. When I first started People In Progress Pty Ltd I had $167 in my wallet, no job and a spare bedroom as my office. I used a $25 card table as a desk for a long time, had an old second-hand computer held together by a rubber band and a big yellow book filled with potential clients – the Yellow Pages! I was new to Sydney so I literally had no contacts and no network to help me. So I sat on that phone every day – calling, calling, calling – being rejected, day after day. Then it happened. Someone said, 'Yes! I'll see you!' Nothing comes easy and if I worried about 'looking good' I would have never had the guts to put myself out there to be rejected so many times.

2. *The lack of sacrifice and not wanting to do the hard yards* – so many people want all of the trappings of success but are not willing to do whatever it takes to get there. It takes serious hard work to be successful at anything; there are no short cuts. There is a lot of talk these days about accelerated learning but I believe there are some things you can't and shouldn't accelerate. I have always pushed harder, worked longer, just kept moving forward even when everything in me wanted to stop. I can honestly say that I have never allowed my feelings to get in the way of what needed to be done. Nerves, sickness, tiredness, insecurity, heartbreak, fear – I just keep doing what needs to be done in all parts of my life and in the end the results are there.

What are some of your goals for the next five years?

From a business perspective, I would love to continue presenting on speaking circuits. I also have some great plans for People In Progress over the next few years, which include further growth of the training side of the company, and an online presence for the business called, People In

Progress Interactive. Now that I have completed my first book, *There Are Only Two Times in Life...*, I am following it up with a series of children's books called, *Stickman Rules*. I am also producing a clothing line next year with a friend. On a more personal level, I plan to take my boys on some really exciting holidays, which we are all looking forward to doing.

What do you love most about being where you are today?

I love that my choices and decisions are not influenced by what other people think of me. The wonderful thing about getting older is that you start to trust yourself a lot more and as much as I'm constantly looking for teachers and role models, I don't need other people's approval to feel good about myself. I have also worked very hard for a lot of years and am now financially independent. As a woman, this has allowed me to make very different choices, which is very liberating.

Lauren Burns

LAUREN BURNS

66 It was a close fight but this time I came away
the winner. Looking back I know that if I hadn't
lost to her at the World Championships I
probably wouldn't have had the tactical skills to
beat her at the Olympics. 99

LAUREN BURNS

Growing up with a pop star for a father, a dancer for a mother, attending Preshil (an alternative school) and making the choice to become a vegetarian at the age of three, it is surprising that Lauren Burns found her passion in the full-contact martial art of Taekwondo.

Lauren created sporting history by winning the first-ever Olympic gold medal for Taekwondo when the sport made its debut at the Sydney 2000 Olympic Games. She was one of only three Australian women to win an individual Olympic gold medal, along with Cathy Freeman and Susie O'Neill. Her amazing triumph at the Sydney games was achieved against the odds – requiring enormous discipline, commitment, perseverance and teamwork.

Since retiring from Taekwondo after the Sydney Olympics, Lauren has become one of Australia's most sought-after speakers. In her presentations she talks about what it takes to be successful, and transforms her stories and experiences into life skills making them entertaining and relevant to her audiences.

Lauren interacts with her audience with the added highlight of inviting someone up on stage to break a board. And during her more active workshops Lauren has the entire audience breaking boards! Her presentations always leave the audience buzzing with excitement.

Applying the same enthusiasm she had for competitive sport, Lauren is currently studying at the Australian College of Natural Medicine where she is completing a Bachelor in Health Science (Naturopathy).

Lauren enjoys a variety of commitments, however, her main focus within the community is her involvement with Red Dust Role Models, conducting healthy lifestyle clinics in remote Aboriginal communities. She is also a director on the board of Appin Hall Children's Foundation. Lauren is currently also on the Athletes Commission of both the Australian Olympic Committee and Taekwondo Australia.

When did your love affair with Taekwondo begin?

I began Taekwondo when I was 14 years old after my brother Michael did a flying side kick through the lounge room window. He was seven at the time and fancied himself as a Teenage Mutant Ninja Turtle – so much so that the family had to call him Donatello otherwise he wouldn't respond. My mum enrolled him in the local Taekwondo centre, which he loved and soon after my dad began too. They would come home and practise in the lounge room and always encouraged me to join them. One day I finally did, but this wasn't where the love affair began. I started attending classes twice a week and there was something about the continued learning and the achievements of each grading that I enjoyed. Then one night my instructor announced he had entered some competitors into the Victorian Championship that coming weekend and I was one of them!

I recall entering the championship with no idea of what to expect and being bombarded with the most incredible cacophony of sporting sounds – horns, whistles, people yelling and screaming, six courts running all at the same time. My mum, from a classical ballet background, took one look around and said, 'Lauren, there's no way you are fighting – these people are crazy!' mainly referring to the cheer squad (made up of parents, coaches, friends and family) that surrounded each court.

My fight was late in the afternoon. I had been nervous all day but when I finally stood next to my opponent I was overwhelmed with fear. Fear that I would not be able to kick, that I wouldn't be able to move my legs. Suddenly my legs felt like dead weights. In a blur, my instructor pushed me into the ring and the referee started the fight. The total opposite happened – I couldn't stop kicking! I was doing everything I could remember: head kicks, spins, fancy kicks, anything I could think of. She was doing the same – we were both going hell-for-leather but neither of us was actually touching the other! Within the first 30-seconds we were both exhausted. We leant on each other, then started kicking again. These sporadic bursts of action continued for the first two rounds.

66 During sparring it was down to business, no-more-Mr-Nice-Guy! 99

In the third and final round, she executed a kick that just clipped my face. I tasted blood! Although at the time I didn't realise that it was only a tiny cut on my lip, all I could think of was 'There is BLOOD IN MY MOUTH!' It was the first time I had ever taken a kick to the face and as the referee gave me the eight count, all I could see out of the corner of my eye was my mum, burning down the stairs screaming, 'Go Lauren! Kick her in the head!' just like the other people she thought were crazy only hours earlier.

I came home thinking that competitive Taekwondo was not for me, but as the evening wore on I could not ignore the fire burning in my belly. I wanted to be better and I wanted another chance to prove to myself that I could win the state titles. I knew I could improve, particularly considering I had entered that competition not even knowing the rules. I began to train with my friend at the club, Donna Scherp. This was when my real love affair with Taekwondo began – the buzz of training, the feeling of improving, the adrenaline rush of hitting the mark or nailing a complicated kicking routine. The incredible endorphin rush of hard physical exercise and the application of all skills during sparring and competition were both challenging and exhilarating at the same time. These feelings were unparalleled to anything I had ever experienced and I threw myself into training with an excited fervour.

Starting out, what were some skills you were lacking and what did you do about it?

Technique and experience. When I first started competing I had average technique and no ring experience. I went to an alternative school called Preshil and having never played competitive sport before had no idea *how* to train. But once I became serious about Taekwondo I began training with Donna who turned out to be an ideal partner. She had a strong background in competitive sport and encouraged me to use video footage to assess our progress. We regularly set up a video camera to film ourselves practising every kick we knew. We would then watch them back and critique ourselves.

This technique is used by athletes and sporting institutes all over the world. Years later I used this video technique again when visited by Seung Min Lee, the featherweight world champion from Korea. She joined us at a training camp at the Australian Institute of Sport (AIS) and the technicians filmed her kicking. I obtained a copy and compared my technique to hers. Her execution was beautiful and her technique was flawless – it was an incredibly valuable exercise. By improving technically and gaining fighting experience as we trained and competed all over the world, our other skills then evolved such as confidence, match management and overall awareness of the game.

When things became serious you frequently travelled to Korea to train with the world's best. How did this change you as a person?

Korea had a huge impact on my life. It is the birthplace of Taekwondo and the Korean athletes have been dominant on the world stage for a long time. The main benefit of training there was to provide isolation and the ability to focus purely on training and recovery every day without distraction. Also, in Australia we don't have anywhere near the numbers of people practising Taekwondo so we lack the volume of sparring partners. For instance in Melbourne I trained each night with the national team and there were only two or three other girls who were in my weight division. In Korea I could walk into any high school or university training hall and find at least five world-class girls – just in my weight division. It wasn't uncommon to jump in a taxi and start talking to the driver, who would happen to be a Third Dan Black Belt. The most important aspect about my time in Korea (other than developing an absolute love for the food) was the intensity and commitment devoted to training. Their training sessions were very physically demanding. During sparring it was down to business, no-more-Mr-Nice-Guy! I wasn't used to this atmosphere at first (no laughing in class or smiling either), but I got used to it and relished those sessions, learning a great deal from each class. Of course, in true Korean style, karaoke was a common occurrence at the end of a hard session.

Leading up to the Olympics, what did your training schedule look like and how was your diet?

My training schedule looked like this:

- *Morning training (6.30am)* – either weights or swimming.
- *Walking* – two hours every day (for recovery and cutting weight).
- *Evening training* – a two-hour session (arriving an hour early to warm-up). Afterward I would walk to the aquatic centre for a hydrotherapy recovery session. I was only really diligent with my recovery in the year leading up to the games and the difference was significant, especially in relation to stiffness the next day and a marked decrease in injuries.
- *Saturday* – usually an individual session where we could practise whatever we wanted. I would also do two to three other individual sessions per week.
- *Wednesday nights* – no Taekwondo training, instead I went to a yoga class.
- *Sunday* – was a rest day, except for walking.
- *Video analysis* – although not physical training, I consider watching fights as important as any physical session. I would watch my own fights and particularly focus on the ones where I had done well. Mostly though, I watched fights of my competitors and other athletes who inspired me.

My diet usually looked like this:

- *Breakfast* – porridge (with nuts, sultanas, maple syrup or honey) or good quality toast with avocado, lemon juice, pepper and sprouts.
- *Lunch* – a big bowl of steamed vegetables with Napoli sauce and cheese, or spelt or wholemeal pasta with vegetables and tofu, brown

rice, legumes, vegetable stews and curries, or a big salad with green leafy vegetables, egg, legumes, nuts and seeds.

- *Dinner* – vegetable soup, steamed vegetables, fresh juice or a smoothie (with banana, LSA mix, honey, flaxseed oil).
- *Snacks* – fruit, fresh raw nuts and sultanas.

As weight divisions are a crucial element of Taekwondo, how important is dieting?

Diet and nutrition have always been important to me. I have been vegetarian since I was three years old and have always been passionate about food and healthy eating. Kids at school thought I was strange bringing along seaweed strips or a bag of brewers yeast flakes. It took time to achieve the right balance when incorporating correct nutrition into my training regime. Taekwondo is a sport consisting of weight divisions. I usually dropped weight to fight in the under 51kg class. For the Olympics I dropped even more to fight in the under 49kg class.

Over the years I have subjected myself to various forms of dieting torture – saunas, sweats, not eating for days, severe dehydration – all the while knowing the affect it was having on my body and my brain. Being even slightly dehydrated results in an inability to think quickly, make split-second decisions and tactical judgements. In the past I've found myself in full head-to-toe sweats skipping off those last few hundred grams in a car park in Belgium, or kicking frantically to raise a sweat in the sauna at the Northcote YMCA while three overweight old men watched on in disbelief. The more I developed as an athlete the more I was determined not to employ any of these archaic forms of weight-loss and became fastidious with my diet. One of my greatest sponsors was Dynamic Vegies, an organic fruit and vegetable store that kept me supplied with wonderful fresh produce and nutrition. Although I am talking about dieting, it wasn't about a

> 66 For the Olympics I dropped even more to fight in the under 49kg class. 99

reduction in food but rather the way I structured my eating and the quality of the food I consumed. I actually ate a lot more back then compared to how much I eat today, but I was also doing seven hours of physical activity each day.

My focus was on good quality organic and biodynamic produce and an abundance of fruit and vegetables. I tried to be creative and come up with ways of cooking that focused more on steaming and grilling and leaving the ingredients in their freshest state. I avoided heated oils and trans fats, and instead added quality oils (olive, flax, sunflower, sesame seed, evening primrose, oat bran and rice germ) to my salad dressings and to meals just before serving. These oils contain Omega 3, 6 and 9 fatty acids. I ate nuts, avocados and combined various legumes and rice.

When I was training for the Olympics the major aspects of my diet included a substantial breakfast followed by the main meal in the middle of the day which was usually a huge bowl of steamed vegetables with lentils and Napoli sauce. Training would finish too late for a large meal so I would have something immediately after finishing, like a banana or some nuts or brown rice and then something light for dinner like soup, a smoothie or fresh juice. Due to the high intensity and sheer volume of training I often found I craved sweet foods. Mostly I tried to be innovative and create recipes that satisfied my sugar craving but were nutritious at the same time, such as baked apples with walnuts and honey or sprouted bread toasted and topped with jam and tahini.

An important aspect of dieting, as anyone who has been on a 'diet' will know, it's not only about the foods you consume – it's what you're *not* eating! Suddenly you crave things you would never dream of simply because you know you can't have them. The mental challenge is often the most difficult. For this reason I never denied myself my biggest weakness – chocolate – mainly to prevent binge eating but just knowing that I could have some when I wanted it meant that I didn't eat it often. When you have a myopic focus about something you need to have some leniency and flexibility. Having single-minded determination is imperative in competitive sport but being too rigid and obsessed can work against you.

These principles of nutrition and eating vital, whole, living foods are still values that I uphold today. As our society grows more toward highly processed, packaged and genetically modified foods it is becoming even more important that we remain conscious, awake and aware of our food choices.

Did you ever dream that you would get to compete in the Olympic Games let alone win gold?

The first time I ever gave any thought to going to the Olympics was when I was eight years old and was going to ride horses with my cousin, Narelle. As the intention was for both of us to win gold at the same time we decided to create an event just for us – the double bareback! During my teenage years the thought of being an Olympian never crossed my mind. However, when it was announced that Taekwondo would be included as a full medal sport in the Sydney 2000 Olympics I promised myself I would do everything in my power to make the team. Ranked number one in my division two years prior to the games, I felt I could win a medal. But in the months prior there was no question about it – I was going to win gold. I don't think you can win a major event like the Olympic Games unless you believe in yourself and believe you can.

After the media frenzy died down you had hundreds of offers to help charities. What did you decide to do?

What happened after the games was life changing. I never anticipated the media attention or the requests that came. In fact I was struck by the numerous charities out there and the wonderful work that people are doing in the community. Totally overwhelmed with offers I decided that I could make more of an impact by focusing on one or two charities that I was passionate about.

Destroy a Minefield Rebuild Lives – I became the ambassador for World Vision's Destroy a Minefield Rebuild Lives campaign in Cambodia, which allowed me to visit the country and see the destruction and ongoing terror that landmines cause and leave in their wake. Four to six million landmines are still randomly scattered throughout Cambodia and this campaign aimed to raise money to clear land for community sites to be built. Being a part of this program gave me enormous hope. Returning a year later and seeing the school, nursery, and healthcare centre all in place as a result of money donated by Australian people was inspiring.

66 Four to six million landmines are still randomly scattered throughout Cambodia... 99

Red Dust Role Models – I am now involved in this program where various people (athletes, musicians, and so on) tour remote Aboriginal communities sharing healthy lifestyle and educational messages using sport and music as the vehicle for communication and interaction. Being involved in the tour is incredibly rewarding and being invited into communities and welcomed by the kids is immensely gratifying and humbling.

Appin Hall Children's Foundation – Supporting children with serious illness. This is my parents' organisation in Tasmania. Although I am not involved in this foundation on a daily basis I am on the board of directors and am constantly inspired by their commitment to children and their vision of building a more loving and harmonious environment for future generations.

What do you think are the essential qualities or personal attributes of a successful person?

- self-belief
- confidence
- passion
- focus (the ability to keep the vision in mind when times are tough)
- to be unafraid to make mistakes

- creative intelligence, the ability to think laterally and innovatively
- willingness to take risks
- responsibility for their actions
- action – success is in the doing. A lot of people don't move past the talking, dreaming and planning stage.

Have you ever experienced a low point in your sporting career? Can you tell us what happened?

It was during the 1999 World Championships in Canada. I was ready – training better than I ever had before. Having been to the last three championships and with plans to retire after the Olympic Games in 2000, this was my last shot to reach my long-term goal of winning a world championship. It was my time, and I was sure of it.

My first fight went well – I won 12-1. My next fight was against the current world champion, Chi Shu Ju from Chinese Taipei. The fight was close and ran at a draw for most of it with the tension and concentration thick between us. Each time one of us scored a point the other would score straight away and with a few seconds to go in the last round it was still a draw. Attempting to seal the decision and to show aggressive match management (a factor taken into consideration by the judges in case of a tie), I attacked. She countered and scored. The decision went to Chinese Taipei which then went on to win the tournament.

Even at world championship level, Taekwondo is not seeded so the draw can have a huge impact on results. Because I fought Chi in the second round I walked away from that competition with no medal, no ranking, and some shining bruises. Feeling at a complete low after the fight I mustered up the strength to sit in the stands, recording Chi's fights throughout the day. Dejected and miserable I had no idea how handy those tapes would be during the course of the following year. When I got back to Australia I watched those videos hundreds of times. I picked her apart, studied her every move, and simulated her in training. She became my focus. If I could beat her, I could beat anyone. As fate would have it, my first fight at the Olympics was Chi Shu Ju. It was a close fight but this time I came away the winner. Looking back I know that if I hadn't lost to her at the World Championships I probably wouldn't have had the tactical skills to beat her at the Olympics.

Every challenge we have leads us on a different path. We are human beings and we will all have events in our lives that continue to challenge us. Some challenges are bigger and more difficult than others but I believe that it is the way we deal with them that makes us who we are and gives us the ability to move forward and grow. Often it is the challenges that we face or the mistakes that we make that change us, give us clarity or allow us to look at our life from a different perspective.

Were there any times when you wanted to give up? What got you through?

There were times in my Taekwondo career when I really questioned whether I wanted to continue. Once, years before the Olympics, I had both knees operated on at the same time. I had one leg in a full leg splint for a month and was immobile for some time. The rehabilitation was painful, drawn out and tedious. One day I thought 'Hey, why am I doing this to my body? I don't have to do this anymore if I choose not to'. Other than my own expectations and those of my coaches, I had no obligation to continue competing. I certainly wasn't getting paid to train. I was doing it for the love of it and frankly, it just wasn't fun anymore. Once I allowed myself the option of stopping, I realised how much I really wanted to compete again. I loved Taekwondo and I wanted to get back to the level I was at before the surgery, but I obviously needed this down time to refocus and re-energise my determination.

There were people who helped geet me through. My strength coach, Tony Hewitt, worked with me daily on my rehabilitation, re-enforcing that this particular time was vital as he would assist me in becoming stronger than I was before. The other person who made a huge difference was my friend Sally, whom I was living with at the time. She always made me laugh which was the best medicine and helped me to not take it all so seriously.

In hindsight, most of the challenges and times when I considered giving up usually resulted in making me stronger in some way mentally, physically, spiritually or emotionally. This is indicative of most challenges in life. It's how you deal with them and how you learn from them that makes the difference.

Is there a significant quote or saying that you live by?

Follow your passion and excitement in life. I believe it is the fire and enthusiasm that you feel when you're excited about something which leads you in the right direction.

A favourite quote is one I read recently in the book *Wall and Piece* by Banksy: '*A lot of people never use their initiative because no one told them to*'.

And then there are my *Star Wars* favourites:

'*Many of the truths that we cling to depend on our point of view*' – Obe-wan Kenobi

'*Try not. Do. Or do not. There is no try*' – Yoda

Who are the role models or mentors that have inspired you? What important lessons have you learnt from them?

I think I sought out mentors long before I even understood the term 'mentor'. I have always been interested in other people's journeys and I believe that you can always

66 I think I sought out mentors long before I even understood the term 'mentor'. 99

learn something from somebody else – even if it's how you *don't* want to do something. There are so many experts and talented people out in this big wide world, why not draw on their expertise and experience?

Some of the people that have inspired me include:

Tony Hewitt – my strength and conditioning coach who challenged my thinking and educated me in understanding my body and the training methods that would facilitate improvement in speed, power, flexibility and agility. He also understood the mentality and traditional elements of martial arts.

Deidre Anderson – from the Victorian Institute of Sport taught me about how to help people come to a decision they already know within themselves. She gave me this gift on many occasions, gently encouraging me to trust my own intuition. She has the ability to ask the right questions, to listen and to assist someone in finding the answers they are looking for. Also, she is a can-do person. She always finds a way to make things happen, through thinking laterally and exploring creative options for problem solving.

Jeff Simons – the sports psychologist who travelled with us in the years leading up to the Olympics. His advice still rings in my head – 'Do the simple things with excellence'. This is applicable in so many fields of endeavour.

Do you believe winning is everything?

When I was competing, winning competitions was everything. Outside the ring I am not a competitive person. Driven – yes, but I don't have a competitive 'win at all costs' attitude in the way I approach things. I like to push and challenge myself, but after retiring from competitive Taekwondo I look back on my journey and can see that it was the pursuit of winning and always striving for the Olympic ideals – faster, stronger, higher – that actually helped me to grow and develop as a person.

What lessons have you learnt from Taekwondo that now apply to other areas of your life?

- Natural talent is not the cornerstone of success. Passion, excitement, commitment and hard work are more important.
- Trust your intuition.
- Prepare well and take considered risks.
- The power of silence – take time to be still within yourself and get in touch with your inner strength by *being* with yourself.
- 'Fake it 'til you make it' – how would you think and behave if you were the person you want to be? By changing your actions and physiology, and reconditioning your thoughts and reactions to be the person you want to be you can initiate long-term change. My coach used to ask me 'How would you fight if you *were* an Olympic Champion?' I realised I was always training as if I had someone to beat, not as if *I* was the person to beat. You'd be surprised how quickly you can change your state.

What strategies do you use to remain focused under immense pressure?

- Remembering and concentrating on the things within my control.
- Going over and re-enforcing the things that I know I can do well.
- Simplifying things.
- Taking one step at a time. Often immense pressure can be overwhelming. I like to bring things back to focus on bite-sized pieces while still keeping the big picture in mind.

You now do a lot of public speaking. What are some of the key messages in your presentations?

You don't have to have natural talent to be successful – often we feel that if we're not naturally good at something we can't succeed in that area. I believe that if you love what you do, have passion and excitement, and are not afraid to put in the hard work then you can do anything. Natural talent only gets you so far. It is enthusiasm, hard work and the ability to keep going when you have setbacks that are the ingredients for success.

It's not the challenge you face, it's how you deal with it – challenges come from all directions, be it family, business, or sport and they happen to all of us. Some people face setbacks with a positive outlook no matter how bleak the situation seems, while others let even the smallest inconvenience weigh them down. Some of my biggest challenges took me one step back and two steps forward. These times can propel you toward a huge learning curve. It's a mind-set, it's how you choose to live, think and behave.

Simplicity: doing the simple things with excellence – this was always reinforced by my sports psychologist. There was a time in Korea when I was sparring with a young high school boy. Every time he kicked, he did a back leg roundhouse kick (the most commonly used kick in martial arts) and each time he scored against me. After failing in my attempts to score, I decided that instead of countering his kick I would simply focus on fast footwork to move out of the way. Still he scored each time. This story demonstrates the power and beauty of one simple technique being executed so perfectly that it was unbeatable. Even though I *knew* what kick he was going to do and I could *see* him coming, I still couldn't get out of the way. I find this concept inspiring as it applies to many fields of endeavour. For example, businesses often get so caught up in the complexities of running a business that they forget about the customers. Human beings often focus on *all* the things they need to improve, rather than perfecting the things they're good at and can make an impact with.

What advice would you give to other women still searching for that thing they love to do?

For me, love is paramount. I had an immense, burning passion for Taekwondo, for training, travelling, competing and always wanting to be better. I don't have the same feverish passion about any one thing in my life at the moment but I have simply turned my drive from competitive sport and channelled it into other areas. I got enormous satisfaction from writing my autobiography, *Fighting Spirit,* in 2001 and I am currently focusing my energies on studying at the Australian College of Natural Medicine where I am completing a Bachelor in Health Science (Naturopathy). I am far more balanced in my approach these days and spend more time with friends and family.

I use passion and excitement as a barometer – if I have a connection with something and it really excites me then I know I will have the energy to make it work. My advice for those searching for their passion is don't focus on the end result or dismiss something because it is inconvenient, impractical or doesn't make you any money. These are common reasons why people don't pursue the things that bring them joy. You never know where something will lead you. If you have an inkling of something you love doing (whether it be stargazing,

66 It's a mind-set, it's how you choose to live, think and behave. 99

jelly wrestling, gardening, rocket science or taking a peaceful walk) then set time aside each week just to focus on doing that thing. When you give yourself the opportunity to feel excited, passionate and exhilarated you are often far more productive in other areas.

There was a study conducted where people on their deathbed were asked the two biggest regrets they had in life. On the top of the list was 'not spending more time with family' and second was 'not taking more risks'. This world is an amazing and diverse place – you never know what might happen if you get out there and give life a go!

Lisa ♡

LISA
MCINNES-SMITH

66 It is important that we believe in ourselves
so that we can believe in our capacity to achieve
something. I often ask people this question: Why
not you and why not now? 99

LISA
MCINNES-SMITH

Lisa McInnes-Smith was born in Sydney in 1959. She was born without muscles in her left eyelid and was unable to open her eye until she had undergone several operations. Throughout her childhood Lisa was made fun of by other kids, but it developed her resilience and determination.

Lisa's family were all determined. Her mum and dad were determined to build a better life, and her two brothers were determined to play tennis at the top level. These dreams and many others were all achieved. Her family's achievements inspired Lisa to study sports psychology and the psychology of achievement.

At 26 years of age, and in a period of hardship once again, Lisa set her biggest goal: to positively affect the lives of one million Australian teenagers. It was a goal that was to change her life. In the eight-and-a-half years it took to achieve her goal, Lisa travelled the country speaking in schools and to youth groups. Parents of those young people, also inspired by what they heard, invited Lisa to speak in their places of business, establishing her as an inspirational corporate speaker. The rest is history.

Lisa is now recognised among the top inspirational speakers in the corporate sector and speaks on stages around the world. She has written seven best-selling books and presented to over one million adults! Her influence has been recognised through her induction into the International Speakers Hall of Fame, the only person outside North America to achieve this recognition for excellence.

Lisa lives with her husband Colin, is the mother of three children and remains passionate about seeing lives changed for the better.

How did growing up in a family of high achievers affect your life?

I was surrounded by professional tennis players. My father was a professional and my brothers were international circuit players. My mother had the knack of turning whatever she undertook into gold. Although my parents came from poor backgrounds they had a great belief in their ability to build a better future and it permeated throughout the whole family. I remember writing a story in grade three on how I wanted to be a success just like my mum. She was my hero.

My parents created a positive environment. My two brothers and I grew up believing we could be whatever we wanted to be, and that hard work was a happy part of life. We would sit around the kitchen table sharing our dreams on a regular basis. Mum and dad often stimulated us to think about the future and how we'd like to create it. My parents indirectly influenced everything I did. My mother taught me to treat everyone with respect no matter how they appeared, and that everyone was of equal value. My father taught me that my word was my bond. This helped me to think before I promised, and to carry through on what I said I'd do. Underpinning their high achieving mentality was a standard of integrity that wasn't to be compromised, and I caught it.

What is the most important thing you have learnt about being a mother, wife and businesswoman?

Being a mother is the most revealing role that I've ever undertaken, as my children reveal all my weaknesses. I thought being married revealed all my faults, but children magnify each and every weakness and uncover new ones! A child will take as much of you as you are willing to give. In fact, a child will take all of you and leave nothing for anyone else, if you allow it. This is an important lesson – how do I balance babies, husband, work and self?

One of the hardest lessons I learnt was that only I could look after me. I needed to define what it was that I needed for good health, clear thinking

> **66 I'm not perfect, but I am perfectly suited for my children and their needs. 99**

and a happy heart. What refuelled and encouraged me? What could remove me from the baby doldrums? What would it take to get me out of my nightie and out the front door when I had slept so little? Motherhood is a master juggling act. The problem is knowing what to juggle and what to let drop. I felt tired all over and at times just wanted to sleep, feeling bereft of anything to give anybody. This is not exactly an inspiring picture, but motherhood is a wake-up call. It is an opportunity to leave your selfishness behind and become more than you ever dreamed you could be.

I learnt I could do more than I thought. I could juggle more roles and meet more needs simply because they were there in front of me. I wrote out a list of all the roles that I was trying to play –mother, wife, friend, daughter, sister, housekeeper, cook, taxi driver, counsellor, nurse, businesswoman, business partner, client relations. It was impossible to do all these roles well, so something had to give. My job was to choose which areas were priorities, and lower the expectations of myself in the other areas.

My choice of self-talk became incredibly important. I had to build myself up and encourage myself daily. A dear friend reminded me that I was the perfect mother for my children. I'm not perfect, but I am perfectly suited for my children and their needs. That's why God chose me! My job was to get on with it with the best attitude possible. My self-talk was determining my attitude. It's amazing how most character development happens in your own home, like how you speak to yourself when you're in the kitchen trying to juggle meals and children, or how you speak to yourself in the bedroom when you're exhausted but your husband wants a little of your time! I have learnt that positive thinking is not everything, but it is definitely a lot better than negative thinking, and a lot more empowering. I learnt day-by-day that my world was shaped by the words I chose to say to myself. What I said, I did. What I said, I became. What

I spoke out loud was my world and I needed to guard my words very carefully. This was also something important to teach my children.

After some time working you had a turning point in your life. What happened?

My early working life encompassed many different careers over a relatively short period. While finishing my human performance degree I coached swimming and tennis and did catwalk modelling. I then taught French and physical education while deciding if I should do further study. I loved teaching but knew that it would be difficult for me to flourish in the confines of the system so I left to venture into new opportunities, but found that nothing satisfied my soul.

It was at this point that I was confronted with a Christian message and it seemed so simple – love God and love others. I wanted to know what loving God was like. I knew how to love others because my parents had loved me completely and unconditionally. I knew love wasn't just about feelings, it was about commitment and making personal sacrifices for the sake of others. It seems funny that a sense of purpose came to me after praying the very simple prayer 'God, if you love me enough to do something with my life, you can have it'. Everything in my life changed when I realised that God *did* have a plan and purpose for my life. I began to realise that life wasn't all about me. I felt as if I was directed to focus on people I could help – teenagers. I knew a great deal about goal setting, problem solving and self-esteem and I felt compelled to share it. It's interesting how God doesn't ask us to do things that we are not capable of.

I started to record practical information and inspiration on goal setting and problem solving. When my brother said that it needed a few work sheets to complement it I added 80 pages! Suddenly I had a program called 'Why Wasn't I Told?' that any young person could listen to and work through. The feedback was phenomenal and requests came from schools everywhere to speak about goal setting and problem solving. It was so satisfying taking encouragement to town after town. It also showed me that where God leads he also opens a door and makes a way.

How have your Christian values and beliefs affected the way you run your business and your life?

Our business is run the same way we run our personal lives. We've chosen to serve and benefit other people, not ourselves. We commit to providing excellent value each time we serve our clients and we endeavour to have them delighted by their time shared with us. Although we're employed to influence a whole audience, the audience is made up of hundreds of individuals who need to see consistency in our one-on-one interactions with them. What happens over a conversation at a cocktail party is just as important as the message delivered from the stage.

Our marketing strategy is a little different to most. We pray about which clients we will work for and which engagements to accept. We can't do everything, so we need some divine wisdom in most situations. We look for and anticipate signs of guidance and it seems that God's marketing has been very consistent for the past 20 years! Others might say it's a coincidence.

A high level of integrity is required in our business as we learn so much about the inner workings of each company that engages us. Trust is one of the greatest gifts people can give and we honour that. We put this same trust in God and the words He has spoken, and don't always lean on our own understanding. This has produced fruit in our lives that has far surpassed anything we could have planned.

As a working mother of three, do you struggle to find the balance between your work, family and the other aspects of your life?

Balance is not doing a little bit of everything every day. Balance is not walking on a tightrope while trying to juggle eight different things. Balance is about doing more of the things that count and less of the things that don't. So when it comes to my own balancing act it's much more about priorities and people than about tasks achieved.

Relationships are of the greatest importance to me, so no matter how busy I am with work, I try to give my husband and children the best of me, not what's left of me. I refuse to go out and give my best to strangers and come home tired and cranky to my loved ones. This is where attitude really is a choice. I start the morning happy with my husband and kids and I try to finish my day exactly the same way. We put our family life and goals on the planner first. We mark out family holidays, long weekends away and special time slots where the children might be performing or playing in sporting finals. By doing this we make the most of our work decisions in the bigger picture of our family choices. This way, the kids love to celebrate our successes because they never feel like they are competing with our business.

Who are the role models or mentors that have inspired you? What important lessons have you learnt from them?

My parents are my greatest role models. They each endured difficult family circumstances to build one of the happiest families I know. They started life with so little and built the richest of relationships and a wonderful capacity to share all they have. My mother taught me to treat all people equally – with respect and dignity – and not to put people on a pedestal but to accept them for who they are. My mother did the things that really mattered regardless of whether people were watching her or not.

My dad was a champion tennis player. He was a star as a young man and has continued to compete at the top level throughout his life. My dad taught me about the power of discipline and consistency. It took much dedication to run a business, raise a family and play

66 We can't do everything, so we need some divine wisdom in most situations. 99

championship tennis consistently for over 45 years. Dad's integrity was without question, and if he said he was going to do something he did it. Dad used to take all the kids in our street to the nearby sandhills, on the condition that if anyone played up we would all go home. I tested his stipulation just once, only to discover that we were all promptly brought home. None of the kids were very happy with me, but I learnt a lifelong lesson – I learnt to be as true to my word as my father was.

One of my favourite people in the world is motivational speaker Zig Ziglar (now in his eighties). He continues to affect the business and personal lives of millions of people worldwide. I love the fact that he's the same person off the stage as he is on it. He gives dignity to everyone he meets and doesn't judge people by appearances. He has a magnificent marriage of more than 50 years and works alongside his children in his family business. Not only do his kids like his message, but they like who he is as their dad and co-worker – that's success in my eyes.

Naomi Rhode is a professional speaker who gives her time, energy and expertise to aspiring speakers around the world. While I was on a major American speaking tour – what I thought was the pinnacle of my career – she advised me to go home and look after my babies! She told me there would always be another audience but there would not always be another chance to pour my life into my children. It was very confronting advice, but it was at that moment I chose to be a full-time mum and a part-time speaker. It brought my whole life into better alignment – something shifted in me and I realised that my family needed to come first for my whole life to prosper.

In your experience, why do so many relationships break down?

Many relationships lack the basic ingredient of respect. Respect is something that everybody expects to receive but doesn't readily give. Respect is displayed in the way we speak to one another and in the way we treat one another in the little things each day. What starts off as a doting relationship can often end up as a controlling, demanding or belittling one because of the words or tone used in daily conversations.

A simple statement can come across as a command or become a request purely by the addition of good manners. For example, 'Pass the salt' is demanding whereas 'Would you please pass the salt?' is a pleasant exchange. 'Please', 'thank you' and 'may I?' are the basics of respect. Using good manners on a regular basis is simple, but not easy, because good habits need to be practised daily. Without showing this respect, over time relationships can deteriorate into put downs, name-calling and comparisons. You can get so used to being with someone that you can take them for granted and forget to give them the best of you, rather than the worst.

Respect is intimately tied to trust. It's hard to respect someone that you don't trust. Trust is built by being a person of your word, by doing what you say and by saying what you mean. It's called honesty! When someone doesn't tell the truth – or the whole truth – in the hope that it will appease a situation it brings deception, and deception destroys trust. To maintain a secure, loving relationship, respect and trust need to go hand in hand.

So what five things should couples do to focus on improving the quality of their connection?

Relationships that work well are usually because two people have committed to consistent and ongoing conversation. When couples want to improve the quality of their connection they need to improve the quality of their conversation and often the quantity as well!

A daily ritual – it's good for couples to have a daily ritual in which they share the highs and lows of their day. This is not a problem-solving time, nor a whinge, but simply a time to keep your lover and best friend filled in on the details of your day. It's ideal for it to be over food or drinks where both parties are feeling relaxed and happy.

66 To maintain a secure, loving relationship, respect and trust need to go hand in hand. 99

Practise listening – quality conversation takes place when there is quality listening. Listening is a skill that most of us can improve. Eye contact is essential as well as continual acknowledgement that you are hearing what the other person is saying. The icing on the cake would be your capacity to be able to summarise and repeat back what you have just heard or understood. This acknowledges that you value the person you're listening to, even if you don't understand or agree with what has been said. Being heard makes a person feel highly valued and esteemed.

Asking the right questions – it's easier to listen when you have asked a sincere question that you would like the answer to. Don't wait for your partner to just share randomly but rather be specific with your questions. It also acknowledges that you care about the details in your partner's life.

Schedule time for fun – in the mundane happenings of life, fun doesn't always just happen. We need to make time for fun and plan activities that we both enjoy. We may not share the same interests but we can gain great enjoyment out of participating in something that our partner enjoys. Don't be predictable. Occasionally plan something that's way out of left field for both of you and laugh your way through the process.

Schedule time for intimacy – many couples complain that their love life is lacking. Often this is because it's not on the schedule and it's left to chance. Children and business will take up all of your extra moments so plan for the things that really matter to you! We recommend that couples plan 12 hot nights a year (but not to restrict it to this number!). Give yourself a goal and give yourself a laugh in the process.

Where should people go if they are having ongoing challenges with their marriage or relationship?

Help is sometimes as close as the friends in your life, particularly those in stable, lasting relationships. Most couples need a third party to help them process the topics that cause the most anger or frustration. I don't know where we ever got the idea that what happens at home stays at home. The home isn't much fun to be around if we don't get any help from the outside. There are many couples that have already conquered the challenges that you are facing, and your job is to admit you have a challenge and ask for help. I encourage couples not to wait until their relationship is falling apart or feeling hopeless before they seek help.

There are many resources available today that can further assist you in resolving your challenges. Books are a great place to start, as are DVDs and talking CDs on topics to do with relationships or marriage. Share your feelings with someone you respect and trust. A fresh viewpoint can often help us to think more positively about a solution. Counsellors are a wonderful resource and there are plenty of them, whether they are found through churches or other organisations. The input of an independent person is invaluable. Their experience can put a stop to you going around and around the same problem without progressing. Organisations such as Focus On The Family have wonderful resources and a network of relationship counsellors that anyone can contact. There's also www. troubledwith.com that provides information on relationship issues. You can also visit the Marriage and Relationship Education Association of Australia (MAREAA) website www.mareaa.asn.au, which will refer you to relevant marriage counsellors and courses in your state.

What has been one of the biggest challenges you have had to face in your life and how did you overcome it?

I had been married for eight years and had two children when my husband received a letter from the USA saying he had a daughter who was turning 16 and would he like to acknowledge her? At the time I wished that letter hadn't arrived, and it crossed my mind that we could pretend that it never existed. I felt like we had a hand grenade in the midst of our 'perfect' life and it was about to blow. I wish I could say that I handled it well but instead I told my husband he was ruining our lives. What were we going to do? Would we do anything at all? Our character and integrity were on the line. Was it about us, or was it about a little girl on the other side of the world who just wanted to know her dad? Her name was Kristian and she had longed to know her father all her life. We decided to tell Colin's mother, who was excited at the news and thrilled about having another granddaughter. This response helped me immensely! I had wondered what the family would think, as well as how it would affect our reputation. When we finally got over 'us' and put our focus on Kristian, we knew we had to meet this precious girl.

Kristian kept Colin's first phone message just in case we never arrived so at least she would know his voice. We drove to the south of Florida and when we finally met, Colin was transfixed by this curly-haired blonde who had a definite resemblance to him. I witnessed a miracle as I watched my husband release an abundance of love for Kristian. Something in him just knew that this was his daughter. He had denied it or avoided it for almost 17 years, but now married, a father of two and a lover of God, he had a very different perspective.

For two days they walked the beaches getting to know each other. I waited in a motel room as father and daughter spent much-needed time together. My journey of connection was still to come but I decided in my heart that if this was my husband's daughter then she was equally my daughter. When I married Colin we became one, so his child was my child. I've never called her a stepdaughter, she's simply my eldest daughter. I had always longed for three children and God was giving me my heart's desire. I was extremely grateful. Kristian has changed our lives forever. She spends as much time as she can with us here in Australia and spoils her younger brother and sister. Matthew and Kelly adore her and always greet her with a 'Welcome Home' sign. They were seven and five when they first met Kristian, and she was the best show-and-tell they ever had!

Reunited – Kelly, Matthew, Kristian, Colin and Lisa.

Why are you such a big believer in the power of goal setting?

Goals give you the guts to get going! Goals give you a sense of direction, a target to aim at, a goal to shoot at. It's really hard playing the game of life when you have no idea whether you've scored or not. Everybody needs lots of little goals in all areas of life that matter to them. Most of us set goals subconsciously but if we don't write them down they swim around in our heads like fish in a fishbowl.

People are natural dreamers and goal setting helps to harness the power of a dream and make it come true. When I set what seemed to be the ridiculous goal of positively affecting one million Australian teenagers I'm not sure that I really believed it. But once it was on paper it started to become a possibility. A goal

> 66 I felt like we had a hand grenade in the midst of our 'perfect' life... 99

with a plan and a strategy is a goal that empowers and activates you to action. My big goal was a catalyst to achieve the little goals that would make it possible. It was during the little steps that I often encountered discouragement – speaking to a hundred unruly teenagers was sometimes more than my confidence could take. I would return home telling myself that the goal was too big and too hard and that I was the wrong person. But when I sat and read the goal again, and the 52 reasons why it was worthwhile, my discouragement would dissipate and hope would be left in its place. I would consider having a go, just one more time. That's what goals do. They pull you out of yourself and make you believe that there's more you can do than you really think. Goals expand and enlarge you and challenge you to live up to them. When I was halfway to achieving my goal of one million, I was already thinking about teenagers in other parts of the world!

Even though most people know how important it is to have goals, why do you think so many people fail to set them?

Most people know the theory behind goal setting but their fear is sometimes greater than the excitement of the goal. Some people's lives are run by fear – fear of failure, fear of disappointment, fear of letting people down, fear of success, fear of the unknown. Others thrive on faith, the possibility of success, of overcoming, of succeeding, of making a difference, of making a whole new pathway for themselves. It takes faith to set goals and it takes faith to fight fear. Fear is a formidable foe; it's entangled in our thinking, our beliefs and our thoughts about the future. Fear is what most people think they must conquer before they go after their goals. Funnily enough, goal setting is a pathway to defeating fear. Every step toward the goal pushes fear further away. Competence builds confidence and confidence leads to action. Action achieves goals.

So why is it that so many people fail to set goals?

1. They don't take the time to write them down.
2. They don't make the time to read them.

3. They don't make a plan to reach each goal.
4. They don't write down the benefits of achieving each goal.

All of these steps are easy to do so it just takes a decision to get started and a commitment to follow through.

Why do you say, 'It's the little daily habits that make the difference'?

Once goals are set, it's the small activities achieved day-by-day that take us closer to our goal. It's the small daily habits, not giant leaps, which move us in the direction of our dreams.

Reading a little bit every day in an area of interest makes us more knowledgeable, more interesting and more valuable to the people who want our talents. Most people would prefer to learn from a person who is learning themselves. In fact, when we teach something that we have just learnt, it locks the message into our brain and we get to keep that information much longer. Daily habits of physical or mental health can determine whether we have the energy or capacity to pursue our goals. Most growth needs progressive small steps, so we build on what we've done the day before. A simple habit of getting up half an hour earlier means much greater productivity when we add it up over a year. Many say they'd like to write a book but they never get started, nor do they persevere and keep writing a little bit each day until all their ideas are on the page. Dreams without any daily action are only pipe dreams. Develop the habits that make the difference.

What are some examples of positive success habits one can adopt?

It's important to learn what energises you and what depletes you, what motivates you and what crushes you. Successful people develop a range of successful habits and keep working on new ones. They may include things like personal organisation, doing the important things not just the urgent, learning regularly, showing appreciation for others and nurturing your

> **Simple challenges would bring me to tears and housework seemed a never-ending task.**

spouse, children and yourself! I ask many of my clients to write down the five things that need to be accomplished in any given day that would make them feel successful. Those who feel successful are more likely to tackle the difficult tasks that others never attempt. It is important that we believe in ourselves so that we can believe in our capacity to achieve something. I often ask people this question: 'Why not you and why not now?'

Were there any times when you wanted to give up? What got you through?

Some challenges come when you least expect them. I had just completed the biggest speaking tour of my life, travelling with Colin's parents, two babies and 22 pieces of luggage! I loved every minute of the excitement and adventure of the whole family on the road. As soon as I arrived home, and added the inevitable home tasks to my already busy schedule, I found I was on overload and not able to cope. Simple challenges would bring me to tears and housework seemed a never-ending task.

My husband suspected there was a major challenge when I began shying away from new speaking opportunities. He was used to a wife that could always add one more thing to the list. It was my friends that warned Colin that I was starting to shutdown and shut them out. I was having trouble just making a phone call. I certainly wasn't able to ask for help, and crying was usually my first response. My husband realised the seriousness of the situation when on my last speaking engagement he had to dress me and push me onto the stage. It was the last presentation I did for three months. I went to bed and couldn't get up.

I had two children under two-and-a-half and was no longer capable of taking care of their needs. A psychologist told me I had burnt out, and the maternal child health nurse told me I had postnatal depression. These were both serious diagnoses, and I didn't want to receive either of them. After sharing my journey with my friend and counsellor from church, she declared that I was not burnt out or depressed, but that I was stupid! This was just the diagnosis I needed. I didn't have the answer for burnout or depression, but I could fix 'stupid'.

It took only two months to get back on track after acknowledging that my situation was the result of poor choices. Only I knew what I needed, and if I didn't take care of my own needs, nobody else would. My husband was not a mindreader and could only support my recovery, not create it. We used this time of personal overload to great advantage. We sought counselling for our relationship and restructured the way we lived and worked. I scheduled time for exercise, friends and creative pursuits that energised me. I became more productive and more able to ask for help. I'd been someone who loved to give help but I didn't easily receive it. I was robbing my friends and family of their ability to help me when I needed it the most. This is where I learnt how many people it requires to do anything well. Success is definitely a team effort.

How can we help young women today?

We all have talents and abilities to share and we can choose to walk alongside a younger woman and give her a sense of belonging. We can love and encourage her and choose to believe in her. Girls often need help to work out what is really important in their lives and how they might best pursue it. It's so easy today to be distracted in our world of information, entertainment and endless leisure options. But life is not about leisure – life is about discovering and fulfilling your purpose. There is great pleasure and satisfaction in that, but it's not easy because it takes work and creativity. Girls need to make smart choices, and need help to choose which battles to fight and where to best apply their efforts. Choice requires wisdom and wisdom requires wise counsellors; you become like those you hang around.

A year ago I was approached by a young woman who I have known and loved for some years. She's full of possibilities and she wanted me to teach her how to be an excellent public speaker. I told her that it was easier to teach a group rather than just one, so she drew up the invitation list. Seven excited young women aged between 24 and 36 accepted. I invited them to meet monthly for a year, with the aim of releasing the gifts inside each woman and of growing their ability to positively influence others. My girls soon learnt that there were some significant hurdles to jump in the process – transparency, honesty, trust and forgiveness. Slowly, over the course of the year, the things that held the girls back from their full potential began to dissipate and each one moved to a new and better level of living and speaking.

This is one example of what women can do to help and support younger women. What I did was right in my area of 'gifting'. We all have different gifts. Who knows what might be achieved by just one young woman that you choose to mentor or stand beside?

Cydney O'Sullivan

CYDNEY O'SULLIVAN

66 The float was hugely successful and was considered at the time to be the most successful technology float in Australia. We watched the shares go up every day and when our personal wealth went up to about $60,000,000 I stopped selling at the markets! 99

CYDNEY O'SULLIVAN

Cydney O'Sullivan was born in Venice, California, in the 1960s. She spent her childhood in British Hong Kong, but despite being surrounded by excess and opulence, she had little money of her own and vowed to discover the secrets to creating wealth.

While most of her friends went on to attend prestigious European universities, Cydney's family moved back to California to retire and Cydney found she was only qualified for a job as a restaurant cashier at $3.25 an hour.

Cydney worked her way up the corporate ladder and fell in love with Australia on a visit in 1987. She met and married an Australian, and over the next 15 years they built businesses and had two beautiful children.

When her marriage failed because of money pressures, she decided to get serious about her financial education and taught herself about real estate investing and trading on the stock market from her home office while the children were at school. She now holds multimillion-dollar property, business and stock portfolios and earns millions of dollars through her share trading and investing businesses.

Her latest adventure, the Ms Independence projects, have been created to help other people, women in particular, to learn how to build their own financially secure futures and create wealth through fun interactive programs, books, CDs and workshops (with an emphasis on philanthropic community-building and personal empowerment).

Cydney enjoys writing, water and snow skiing, visiting her friends around the world and hanging out with inspiring people.

You say your life has been a bit of a Cinderella story, why do you say that?

When I was a toddler my dad took us to live overseas and when my parents' marriage failed he left us there and went to live in another country. The split was bitter and I hardly saw my dad again until my late teens. My mum married again and we lived to a schedule that allowed for little idleness (I worked in the family business from a young age and had a lot of chores). My stepfather was extremely tough on me and sometimes he would come home drunk and abusive when Mum was at work. Eventually he gave up the drinking and the violence stopped, but the long hours of work continued. I remember my stepfather constantly telling me that if I moved out I wouldn't make it on my own and because I had heard it my whole life, I almost believed him. But when I was 25 I finally mustered up the courage to move to Australia, and that's when my adult life really began. In fact, I found that I was quite resourceful and took the opportunity to flourish. I found lots of work – at the markets, as a cleaner, as a waitress and shop assistant, and eventually landed a job with a stockbroking firm. Not long after that I met my husband. We had similar dreams, but more importantly, we believed in each other and he encouraged me to open my first business. It was the first of many successes for us and now I can live a bit like a princess. Although my husband was my Prince Charming, the truth is I already had everything I needed to succeed – I just lacked the self-belief.

Having started work at eight years of age, what did you learn about business that you still use today?

Two things: under promise and over deliver, and that personal respect and satisfaction can always be earned from a job well done.

How influential were your parents when you were growing up and in your development as a person?

My dad was a very strong business role model. He was a self-educated CEO who would take over failing companies and make them profitable.

> 66 My mother was very young when she had me and she had to work to provide for us. 99

For a dollar a year salary and a share of the company, he would transform any business. I would have loved to have worked with him, but he didn't believe in giving his children jobs – he saw it as nepotism. It was a shame because I would have loved the chance to get to know him better and sadly, he passed away this year. And it was lucky I didn't hang out for an inheritance as he lost most of his fortune through divorces and the rest on toys. I think seeing the excesses of his spending taught me how easy it is to go through money, even when you have millions.

My mother was very young when she had me and she had to work to provide for us. We mostly looked after ourselves, so I had a lot of freedom. I used to wonder if I was entrepreneurial in spite of my parents or because of them. I think it's probably the latter, because I was so hungry for attention and wanted to prove myself.

In 1985 you were injured in a serious car accident. What impact did this have on your life?

I was a passenger in my friend's car and we were involved in an accident that could have been fatal to both of us. Instead I came out of it with a neck injury that continues to give me problems today. At the moment I'm having a very tough time with constant pain from my neck that runs down my back and arm. It reminds me how close I came to having a short life and so I try to pack as much as I can into every day. My friend and I received insurance payouts for future medical expenses and that few thousand dollars was the big chance I needed to break away from my family and make a life for myself in Australia. I had a friend who was coming to Australia to take a job and she asked me to come along. I was terrified about giving up a really good job as a project manager with an engineering company (although it didn't really suit my personality) and I was afraid of the 'what if...'. Fortunately for me, I had a wonderful boss who told me that if Australia didn't work out, my job would still be there. He also suggested that perhaps this was the best time to leave – no husband, no children and no mortgage to hold me down. He encouraged me to move in a new direction and I haven't looked back since!

Can you explain how you started your first business?

After I decided to start my own business, I went to the library and borrowed books about small business management. There weren't as many then as there are now! Based on my restaurant experience, I quickly decided to start a business involving food, and thought there would be a likely market in Sydney for meals delivered at lunchtime to offices that were isolated.

My plan was to prepare baskets of sandwiches from home and keep my overheads very low, but an experienced friend advised me that it would be best to use commercial premises. I found a place advertised in the newspaper for $20,000, which also included all the equipment and a giant coolroom. The business was a large deli that had been trading for about 20 years before their trading figures became woeful. It was a bargain! There was at least $20,000 worth of equipment and we negotiated the price down to $17,000. The only problem was that we didn't have that much cash. So we arranged finance by selling the equipment to a leasing company for $20,000, used that money to pay for the business and then leased the equipment back on a monthly basis. We got all our friends in and spent a weekend cleaning and painting and used the $3,000 surplus to get the business going. The deli never really picked up, but I found that there was a major demand in the area for catering, and soon my lunch delivery business was bringing in more money than the entire shop's earnings.

Within a year we were doing so much catering that we burnt out. We listed the business for sale and a few months later we had a buyer. We sold the business at a healthy profit, and the return on our investment was especially good when you consider that we didn't even put any of our own money in to start with! We also found that the business lessons we learnt while operating the deli were invaluable considering the amount of money we invested. It was a great grounding for our subsequent businesses.

What did you do after you sold the deli?

After the deli, I wanted to buy a house and back then it was really hard to get a loan. My husband was gaining experience working contract jobs for big corporations and I thought one of us would have to be able to show income stability to get a mortgage. We were also hopeless at saving money in those days and although we seemed to have enough to live on, nothing ever got put away. The classic example was spending all the profit we made on the sale of my business – we took an overseas holiday and paid for our family to come along. We spent the whole year's earnings on one holiday! So I got a job working in the marketing department of a big corporation and stayed there for three years. I also went to adult education (TAFE) classes at night to get a marketing management diploma, which I enjoyed and I am still glad I did it. What I didn't enjoy was the politics of the big corporation and although I had a good job I was feeling very stressed. So once we had our mortgage and bought our house, I started looking around for another business.

You went on to build a number of successful businesses. What were they and how did you manage?

Café – I found a café that had potential but closed down simply because it was poorly run. Before I negotiated a good rental deal, I spent my lunch hours counting the number of customers in nearby eateries and the people passing by, as I wanted to work out how much business I would need to make it viable. Not long after this I set out to reopen the café. It had been completely stripped out, and even though I ruthlessly shopped around for the cheapest fittings, we actually ran out of money and even maxed-out our credit cards. It took months to get the place fitted out, but once we opened I quickly learnt the benefits of a great location, and that new businesses attract customers faster than rundown businesses. We were packed from the first day. We had 60 seats, but the main demand was for take-away food, and when I began advertising catering we were soon doing all of the corporate parties and business lunches too. The biggest problem I had was retaining staff, and we were all working very hard. Within eight months of opening my husband encouraged me to test the market for buyers. Two days later we sold the business at asking price (which was about triple the amount I was earning in my corporate job).

Another café – after a brief break I wanted to do it again and I went into a partnership with one of my friends. She and I had done some catering together and I thought it would be great to have a partner to share the responsibility. Unfortunately, I found that every time I organised to look at premises she would have something else on, and after weeks of her not showing up to meetings I realised that I was lucky to find out early that partnerships can be a big mistake. It's easier to terminate an employee than a partnership.

Catering – I then found out that I was expecting my first child and was ecstatic. I decided that it would be the wrong time to start another restaurant so I placed an advertisement in the Yellow Pages and started doing catering for weddings and parties. This kept me very busy until the baby was born and then I found it too demanding – weddings won't wait and I was trying to prepare feasts with a baby in a backpack!

Baby fashion – I had always loved sewing so I started to make my own baby clothes. Soon friends were ordering outfits for their kids, and I had started a children's clothing business. This suited me well, I could design and sew while the kids were at preschool or sleeping, and I only had to deliver them to shops and sell them at the markets on the weekends. I had a lot of trouble with the shops ordering

66 I only had to deliver them to shops and sell them at the markets on the weekends. 99

stock and then changing their minds, so I took regular spots at monthly markets, and did this for years. I loved seeing the kids at the markets wearing my creations.

Kaz Computers – we had bought shares in the business my husband worked for, Kaz Computers. It was really growing and we were reinvesting the profits for further growth. After about eight years, it had grown from just a few employees to 4,000 and many technology companies were having great success with Initial Public Offerings (IPOs) so we decided to go for it. The float was hugely successful and was considered at the time to be the most successful technology float in Australia. We watched the shares go up every day and when our personal wealth went up to about $60,000,000 I stopped selling at the markets! It sounds like winning the lotto and it was really wonderful, but we were only able to sell small lots of shares at certain times. Company directors usually enter into an agreement to not sell their shares during the first year as it could hurt the share price. Shareholders may also see it as a sign of lack of confidence if the directors are selling out of the company. But when the tech boom became the tech crash a few months later our fortune was almost completely gone – it was such a surreal experience! Fortunately, we had bought some good properties with the proceeds from the float and I was able to improve their value with largely cosmetic renovations. Thanks to the property boom we were making some serious profits on those investments, and over time our shares did get back some of their value.

Costume designs – I soon grew bored of being a 'lady who lunches' as my children were now at school. My kids had always loved dressing up and it was hard to get quality costumes, so I designed a range of children's dress-up clothes. I sold them through agents across Australia to boutiques and toy shops. Orders were slow, so I opened a concept shop that had 'anything magical' as a theme. Soon the shop was packed and we had a good little business going. The pressures of running the shop, designing, manufacturing, stocktaking and wholesaling, together with having a marriage and children to look after were intense. The overheads of running a retail business seemed to be endless and I began struggling to make it worthwhile. My husband was also working incredibly hard and was hardly ever home, and eventually our marriage collapsed. Because of the divorce I had no energy for the business, so I let my staff buy it. It wasn't a very good deal for me and they treated me quite badly, but it was a relief to be able to move on and spend some time healing.

Property – I started reading books about real estate investing and decided to take control of my own finances. I took a gamble and sold the city house at the top of the Sydney real estate boom, and used the profits and mortgage lending to buy a few smaller houses outside of the city and a lovely acreage for my children and I to live on. The plan was to invest in real estate and have a safe future. I looked for family homes that were in need of a serious tidy up, cleaned them up, and rented them out to cover the mortgages as much as possible.

At the age of 41, you had lost a lot of money and your marriage had ended. How did this affect your self-esteem and how did you push through it?

Well, it definitely affected my self-esteem. After being with my husband for 15 years we had made a lot of friends, so it was a shock when we separated and I realised I was on my own. I turned into a bit of a hermit, focused on my education, kept myself very busy with the children, and gradually made new friends. I hated being single again at this age. It was so hard seeing all the skinny young women in the magazines, but I tried not to read them and subscribed to investor magazines instead to improve my financial language.

As a result of lack of experience, my low self-esteem and vulnerability at the time, I did have a few bad experiences with men. In fact, I lost a lot of money investing in businesses with two of them, and loaned money to another who simply refused to pay me back (he preferred to buy himself luxury toys). I even experienced violence from two of them. After these relationships, I worked on learning how and when to say 'no' to people who have money problems. The emotional strain from having these men I loved abuse my trust was very hard to get over. But

> 66 It was so hard seeing all the skinny young women in the magazines... 99

I'm a firm believer in 'what doesn't kill me makes me stronger' and so I focused on learning from those mistakes before moving on. I now have a wonderful support network of friends who share similar interests, a great relationship with my ex-husband, and a very nice man in my life who thinks I'm amazing to have been so resilient. But more importantly, I learnt to be proud of my emotional and intellectual growth and developed a strong relationship with a very important person – me!

After being married for 15 years, what was the hardest thing you had to adjust to?

I think the hardest adjustment for me after being married for so long, and having come straight out of my parents' house into marriage, was the confidence to make my own major decisions. At first it was completely foreign to me. But once I bought my first three properties, organised the paperwork and loans, and created a strong team of advisers with a solicitor, conveyancer, accountant and broker, I started to really enjoy the power of making my own informed decisions. I also find that the knowledge you acquire through your experiences only gets stronger and builds up like a wall of confidence. You might have a financial setback, but you don't lose your experience and your recoveries come much faster and more easily.

Eventually you got into stock market trading. Did you think that it was a risky move?

I'd had experience with many businesses and already had a few rental properties in my investment portfolio, so I was ready for a more risky investment. Share trading was something that I had always thought about and something I believed would be worth learning about as it offered very flexible and lucrative income. So I started looking at shares in businesses that had shown consistently good growth. I like to invest in publicly traded companies so that I can sell my shares quickly and effortlessly, and have always minimised my risks by maintaining a diverse investment portfolio (real estate, business and shares) and by incorporating that diversity throughout my share portfolio as well.

tully ©

What is your definition of wealth?

To me wealth is not all about money. It's about having an abundant, steady and passive source of income, a life and work you love, a supportive community and family, good health, people to love and who love you in return, challenge, adventure and an appreciation of your blessings.

Tell us about your latest business, Ms Independence?

I had a dream of writing for a living and being productive to society. After a year of mentoring with a wonderful friend and entrepreneur,

Anne McKevitt of MillionDollarPlusClub.com, we worked out a plan that allowed me to achieve both objectives, while at the same time helping others live their dream lives. Modern life is getting harder for many people to manage, and money causes a lot more stress than it should because our education system hasn't been able to keep up with the changing times. To address these problems I am creating a series of books, live and recorded workshops, CDs, DVDs and education centres. My first book, *Rich Girls Have More Shoes – a step-by-step guide to money mastery,* will be out soon. We are also running workshops in Sydney, and have now established a membership base that is already in the hundreds. I love the Ms Independence brand so much because it involves working with, and contributing to, a number of productive charities and helping people with their personal empowerment. It's developed from principles I've picked up studying with Robert and Kim Kiyosaki (of the Rich Dad Poor Dad company), Christopher Howard and Tony Robbins, among others. The underlying principle is to empower enough people to make positive change in their own lives, so that they can then go on to help others make similar improvements. The result is a compounding effect that will see thousands of people working toward a better, safer world.

What are the most important things you have learnt about being a mother, wife and businesswoman?

As a mother, wife and businesswoman I've learnt:

- Relationships thrive when you nurture them and wither when you neglect them.
- Being a mother and a businesswoman is a constant priority juggle for me. When I was married I always put my husband's career first, then when I had the children my needs moved even further down the list, but then I discovered that you can and should make your needs a priority too.
- To live how you believe you should not just talk about it. Children need role models to show them how to best fit into society and setting a good example is more powerful than anything you say.

- There are some good things about being a single mother. It is easier because there's only one set of rules in the house and I have the control over what sort of parent I want to be. I also had a lot more time for myself since the children's father took them on the weekends.

What tips do you have for other working mothers to achieve balance?

- Outsource as many of the jobs you don't like as you can – get a cleaner, a gardener, a dishwasher.
- Where possible, plan your days and weeks ahead of time, but be flexible.
- Try and include your children as much as possible so that they can learn from the experience and respect the time you require for work (ask your family and friends to help, but make sure you return the favour).
- Use your time wisely. I used to read books to my kids in the afternoon and evenings when we were all tired. We loved being in the big bed all together enjoying stories and now my children are great readers.
- Make time for yourself, as it makes you happier and everyone benefits.

Were there any times when you wanted to give up? What got you through?

Well, only every time I started a new job or a new business! Will they like me or will they fire me? What if I can't do the job and I look like a fool? If the previous owners failed, why won't I? I used to get this terrible sick feeling that people might reject me, but over time I realised that it's the meaning we give to our feelings that determines the way we react to them. For example, when I started naming the

> 66 The underlying principle is to empower enough people to make positive change... 99

butterflies in the pit of my stomach 'excitement and anticipation' instead of 'dread and fear', I completely changed my emotions. This meant I entered into situations with power, a magnetic confidence and contagious joy of life. Everything is more manageable in that sort of emotional state than when you are worrying about things that are probably never going to happen.

Having said this, my relationship disappointments have been difficult to get through, especially while trying to run businesses and put on a happy face for my children. More than once I've thought I was having a nervous breakdown, and have suffered from depression. I have found regular, long, brisk walks are very good for working through heartbreak and melancholy, and I have a very good support network of friends who coach me through. Neuro-Linguistic Programming (NLP) has also been excellent for working through my insecurities.

As my life has become increasingly more complicated, I have learnt to adopt a big picture attitude and then to break this picture into smaller, more manageable tasks. Now that my businesses are designed to help others to have better lives, I find it a lot easier to get excited about my work. It motivates me to work every day and keep chipping away at my goals. I find it a much more powerful motivator than financial rewards.

Are there significant quotes that you live your life by?

'*Success is not a destination, it's a journey.*' When people are young they seem to want everything to happen now, but you eventually reach a point in your life when you realise that life is going *too* fast! I try to focus on enjoying every day. I have a good belly laugh whenever possible and take the time to experience love every day. I work with friends, travel, choose work that rewards my talents, enjoy my family, and have a big dream that challenges me and keeps me growing. I also have a poster above my desk that says, 'Courage is the ability to make a leap beyond the familiar', and I tend to live by my own motto, 'That which scares me must be done'. My dad always used to tell me to slow down because 'No one ever wished they'd put in more hours at the office when they were lying on their deathbed'. But I believe I would have regretted living a life of fear, wondering who I could have been and what I could have accomplished if I'd only dared to try.

Can you give us your top five business lessons that you have picked up along the way?

1. Choose a business that allows you to do something you LOVE and are GOOD at. Most of us will spend the majority of our lives working, so wouldn't it be great if we could turn it into play?

2. Know the industry and make sure you can make good profits before you start. This will require a plan that covers how you will make a profit in multiple ways and what you will do if the industry changes or competition is introduced. Remember that you can improve your profits by giving your customer more value and it's not always about having the cheapest prices.

3. Plan how you will exit the business, at a profit, before you begin. If you do this you can build the business strategically and exit at a time that suits you best.

4. Be in control of your business, but build a business that doesn't need you and will run smoothly when you aren't there. Put in as many systems as you can so that everyone knows what has to be done and gets it done automatically.

5. Focus on making each stage of your business efficient and profitable before moving to the next one. I have seen many businesses fail because they try to implement too much too soon. I cannot stress the importance of planning out the business and continuously updating the plan on a regular basis.

What advice would you give to other women that are currently experiencing serious financial difficulties?

> **66** If you have debts you have to accept that for a while you'll need to control your spending... **99**

There are thousands of reasons why someone may be in financial trouble. My belief is that nearly anyone can turn his or her life around with commitment and support. The libraries are full of books that you can read to improve your knowledge and there are always jobs that can improve your cash flow. For most people, the habits that got them into bad debts are part of a bigger emotional issue. If you have debts you have to accept that for a while you'll need to control your spending and pay them off, starting with the most expensive. Then you have to chip away at them, gradually increasing your payments until you get them paid off. The Ms Independence website offers a lot of advice for people trying to manage these sorts of issues in their lives.

So what do you think has been the secret to your success?

My brothers seemed to be brilliant at everything. They were always popular and were also stars at sport. Growing up with such achievers instilled in me a competitive, but friendly, desire to win. The big breakthroughs came when I accepted that no one can be the best at everything and began focusing on activities where my investments would return the best rewards, with the results that I wanted.

Another secret to my success is having positive belief systems. I choose to believe that whatever happens in my life is my responsibility and that to blame others is a waste of energy and focus, even though it's normal to want to blame someone else! I choose to believe that I am generally liked, I can learn anything, and that I will always find the resources I need. I also believe that if I tell people what I need they will try to help me.

I've found that it's very powerful to seek out like-minded and supportive friends because they propel you forward. If your group doesn't share your visions and dreams then you can find yourself dragging them along on your journey and that is often very exhausting.

Do you have any regrets? If so what are they?

Just that I didn't have a few more children, and that I spent all those years working in boring jobs simply because I was afraid to go out on my own. I wish I'd started believing in myself years earlier!

FREE BONUS GIFT

Cydney O'Sullivan has kindly offered a FREE BONUS GIFT valued at $29.95 to all readers of this book...

50 Ways To Find More Money! – Cydney O'Sullivan is a successful businesswoman, investor and single mother of two. Having started her first business in her early twenties, Cydney has gone on to develop numerous companies and a multimillion-dollar real estate and share portfolio. Now on a mission to help other women, Cydney has designed a fun and creative e-book full of ideas for finding more cash and securing your own financial future.

Simply visit the private web page below and follow the directions to download direct to your Notebook or PC.

www.SecretsExposed.com.au/inspiring-women

Miriam Schafer

MIRIAM SCHAFER

> 66 In my experience, most people are searching for something, whether it's physical or emotional wellbeing, a desire to feel more connected with their spiritual self, or a deeper sense of meaning or purpose in their life...This can be the time people need the most support. 99

MIRIAM SCHAFER

Miriam Schafer was born in Brisbane, Queensland, in 1959. Growing up with the dream of pursuing a musical career, she also trained in secretarial studies.

When she was 21 Miriam joined the Department of Foreign Affairs and Trade and applied for an overseas posting. Her first assignment was in Beijing. Two years later, she was posted to Nepal to help open the new Australian Embassy in Kathmandu, and later sent to Vienna – the city of her dreams! It was at this point in her life that Miriam immersed herself in music and art and developed a deep belief in the healing power of beauty and pleasure.

In 1990, Miriam joined the United Nations in Vienna, working with the UN Relief and Works Agency for Palestine Refugees. Within five years she was transferred to the Gaza Strip. During this time, despite the challenges of living with danger and an underlying tension, Miriam came to appreciate the richness of the Arab culture, with its warm hospitality and traditions. On the other side of the 'barrier', she spent most weekends enjoying Israel. After 18 months she reached a crossroads in her life and knew that there was something more she needed to be doing. From the Gaza Strip, Miriam moved to New York and enrolled in a four-year course at the Barbara Brennan School of Healing – the world's premier institute of hands-on energy healing and personal transformation.

In 2002, Miriam came home to Australia and set up her Wholistic Life Coaching practice in Noosa Heads. She conducts seminars and workshops in Queensland and interstate, and draws upon nature and design for her inspiration. Her motto in life is *Beauty Heals*.

How would you describe yourself as a person?

I would say I am someone who has chosen to live large and to embrace the challenges that accompany that choice. I've heard it said that at a soul level we decide whether we want to live life on an even keel or on a roller-coaster – I chose the roller-coaster! I believe in past lives, and I believe that I intended in this lifetime to tie up a lot of loose ends from previous ones (for example, with relationships, career and self-worth). It's like I've wanted to have a finger in so many pies! So the essence of who I am is fun-loving and adventurous. I love being with people, and at the same time I love a certain amount of solitude. My journey so far has been one of determination to develop a deeper belief and trust in myself, to overcome an 'addiction to struggle', and to rediscover more of the happy person within.

Your background is very colourful, full of exotic travels and living in six different countries. How has this made you into the person you are today?

This question really resonates with me because I feel like I carry a piece of all of those countries inside me. I think when we live in a different culture a part of it rubs off on us. This has been my experience and when I am reminded of a place where I've spent a significant amount of time, it's like a little flame gets ignited inside and that part comes alive. Sometimes I have felt like a bit of a jigsaw puzzle (made up of lots of different pieces) and in these last four years in Noosa, Queensland, I feel like I've been integrating all these parts of myself, like they've all merged together now. It feels good to have 'come to ground' to allow this integration to take place.

You worked for a number of years with the United Nations (UN), how did this impact you?

I think it really helped me to understand both the diversity of people, and the aspects that are common in all of us. I also learnt about the need

> 66 ...there was still a certain danger factor and a tension in the air. 99

to be tolerant of each other's differences. When you're under one roof with about 40 different nationalities, all doing things the way we think is 'right' it can really be a melting pot, to say the least. There are lots of ingredients going into that soup! Not always a smooth blend, but it's what gives it the rich texture as well. The ongoing impact of the UN days has probably given me a deeper appreciation for people's uniqueness, and this is what I really enjoy about working one-on-one with clients – seeing in them their innate gifts and core qualities, and teasing those aspects out.

What made you decide to live in the Middle East and, as a Western woman, were you treated differently?

I moved to the Gaza Strip because the UN organisation I worked for was relocated there from Vienna in 1996. The UN Relief and Works Agency for Palestine Refugees (UNRWA) had originally been established in Lebanon in 1945 before it moved its headquarters to Vienna. Its mandate was, and still is, 'To provide shelter, health care, education and social services to Palestine refugees, who became homeless in the aftermath of the Second World War'. Land was divided between them and the Jewish people who were seeking a new homeland after coming out of Europe and the concentration camps. Unfortunately, this 'temporary' organisation is still very much in operation today, over 60 years later, because of the ongoing problems in the Middle East and the (now) millions of Palestine refugees that are still in need of basic services. In the mid-nineties there was a new optimism in the region, so the UN Secretary-General at that time directed that this organisation move its headquarters back there. It was an era of real hope for the Palestinians, especially in the Gaza Strip, because it became free from Israeli occupation (despite some ongoing restrictions).

Having said that, there was still a certain danger factor and a tension in the air. There was one fairly major round of ammunition fighting during my time, but apart from that it was more dangerous to be across the checkpoint in Israel, where there were several bomb incidents in cafes.

However I enjoyed my time there immensely, because we moved as one big group of people – friends and co-workers – so there was a lot of support and camaraderie in place from day one. Yes, there were many frustrations. For example, things don't always happen quickly in the Middle East. There is a more laid-back attitude in the Arab culture. When one gets used to it, it's actually very civilised and appealing. Their traditions are rich in hospitality, and this leaves a deep permanent impression. I lived in a charming little bungalow in an oasis-type setting, just a few blocks from the sea. Most weekends I would drive up to Tel Aviv or Jerusalem (both about two hours away) and enjoy the flavour of these cities, either on my own or with friends. In Jerusalem we always stayed at the American Colony Hotel, which had once been a Pasha's residence. It had an amazing history and was a visual delight of blue and green tiled mosaics. In the open-air courtyard, where one dined in the warmer months, there were trickling fountains and lemon trees, swallows darting to and fro, and the scent of jasmine in the evening air (plus the call to prayer from the mosque in the distance). This was a very happy phase of my life.

As a Western woman in the Middle East, it was all relative, depending on where we were. Gaza is quite conservative, so there was a degree of taunting and heckling from the young men on the streets. It was not surprising, as that generation has grown up under very confined and repressed conditions and didn't know better. This is where the underlying tension was quite palpable at times. But it's not so conservative that Western women need to be veiled, as in some other Arab countries. As for the local women, they weren't heavily veiled as such. The majority wore a headscarf with conservative Western clothing. At the other end of the scale in Beirut, Lebanon, many of the local women were wearing the latest Paris fashions, and it was very chic and very liberal! I was actually there last year on a short-term assignment with the UN. I took a few months off from my practice to join this mission. Beirut is truly one of the most romantic cities of the world. Yes, it's troubled and complex, and recent developments have complicated things even more, but it's so very French and stylish. When you combine that with the Arab warmth and hospitality, it's the most wonderful combination. I won't even get started on the food and wine, otherwise I'll never get to the next question!

On a more serious note though, despite the ongoing upheaval in the region, I know of some wonderful programs that are happening, attempting to restore peace at a grassroots level. For example, where Palestinian and Israeli children are interacting with each other and learning about their cultural diversity and similarities, and other powerful stories about organs being donated by Israelis to Palestinians, proving that at the heart of things, many of the people themselves want to heal the rift and live in harmony and unity.

Can you share one or two stand-out stories from your travels?

The first one that comes to mind was during my first posting with the Department of Foreign Affairs and Trade (DFAT), which was in Beijing during the early eighties (in those days it was still called Peking!). For one of my vacations, I took the Trans-Siberian Express from Beijing to Moscow. It was a six-day journey and I was travelling with a friend from the Canadian Embassy. It was one of those deluxe trains with the rosewood panelling and frosted glass – like the Orient Express but not quite as fancy. On about day four, I got left behind at one of the stations in the middle of Siberia. We were having a short stop and the train took off early – I was still buying postcards! Even though it was the middle of summer, there was something rather chilling about finding myself stranded in what felt like no-man's land. This was still during the Cold War and the mood of the people felt very grim. They were also quite suspicious of this foreigner who had kind of dropped out of the sky. It's a story best told over a long dinner party but, in a nutshell, I was looked after very well even though no one spoke English and I spoke no Russian. I was put on the next train to Moscow, and the next day a very charming KGB agent, who spoke impeccable English, showed up out of the blue. She proceeded to wine and dine me all the way to Moscow and I managed to deflect the mild interrogation about 'What do you do at the Embassy?' I reunited with my friend after a couple of days and we had a great time winding down from this little adventure, enjoying the sights of the city.

Another time, I got lost in Rio. I was based in Los Angeles with the Australian Consulate. I was working as the executive assistant to the head of Austrade (Americas), and twice a year I had to organise a conference in a different location for all of our senior trade commissioners based throughout North and South America. So, halfway through the conference week we had a free night with no official function. We were staying at a hotel on Copacabana Beach and I wanted to get over to Ipanema for dinner. I'm a huge fan of Antonio Carlos Jobim and it was a dream-come-true for me to be able to stroll the streets where his music and memory still live on. It was only supposed to be about a 15-minute walk so after about half an hour I started to wonder if maybe I was lost. I kept going for another good while and finally had to admit that I was in fact lost. Usually I have a very good sense of direction, but I think I was so intent on observing all the safety precautions that our security people had briefed us on (that is, don't wear any jewellery, look like you know where you're going and so forth) that I lost track of where I was. Hmmm…well I didn't have a clue where I was and the first person I stopped to ask didn't speak English. When I did find someone to help me, it turned out that I was miles away from my hotel and even further away from Ipanema! Anyway, this isn't such a dramatic story but it illustrated to me at the time that 'people are people everywhere'. There is that basic human quality of helpfulness and trustworthiness, if that is what we ourselves put out into the world. I am often asked, 'Was it scary living here or there?' and I have to say I have pretty much felt safe the world over.

> 66 She proceeded to wine and dine me all the way to Moscow… 99

Do you have a favourite city that you've lived in?

I would have to say New York. There's just something about it – an energy, a vitality – even though it can be an exhausting place after a while. My first impressions of it were that it was like a big commune, so many people packed onto a small island, and needing to get along with each other at close quarters. I really like New Yorkers, they're colourful. Sometimes I felt like I was living in a Woody Allen movie. I lived in three different apartments in less than two years, so I got to know a few neighbourhoods. It's a chapter of my life that represents the worst times and the best times, in terms of my emotional journey and personal growth, so it's a place close to my heart. It was where I turned 40 and in some ways I was just beginning to grow up.

Miriam taking a stroll in Central Park, New York.

What made you turn your back on such a colourful career and head in a completely different direction?

Well, it was quite a gradual process. I guess it began with a basic restlessness, a vague sense that there must be 'something more'. I think discontentment and restlessness are often highly underrated, because when we pay attention to these so-called negative emotions, we can harness them to create positive change. This was the case for me. It was while I was in Gaza that I reached a crossroads. After being there for 18 months, even though the work I was doing was meaningful, I knew it was time to move on. I was working as a personal assistant and looking for new horizons and I had heard about this amazing school just outside of New York called the Barbara Brennan School of Healing. During my years at the UN in Vienna, I was a member of the Esoteric Club and became an avid reader of all things metaphysical, so I had already read a couple of books by Dr Brennan. She wrote *Hands of Light* and *Light Emerging*, which have become classics in the field of complementary medicine. She had been a scientist with the NASA space program and based on her knowledge of frequency, vibration, sound, light, etc, brought it all together with spirituality to create a very comprehensive, holographic healing modality. I wasn't really interested in learning healing techniques at that stage. What attracted me to the program was the personal transformation process that I knew existed. I was hungry and thirsty for a new stage in my own development and the moment I put the wheels in motion, it was as if all the planets aligned and I was on my way to New York. I worked by day at UN headquarters and in my spare hours I got stuck into the course. Needless to say, I also allowed myself some play time in the Big Apple – great jazz, walks in Central Park, the Metropolitan Museum, weekends in the Hamptons…

Over five years of living in the US (two years in New York and three years in Los Angeles) a real metamorphosis took place. The healing school helped me grow in so many different ways. I felt like a reptile whose skin constantly got too tight, so I was continually shedding a lot of old skin. I was building a sense of autonomy, a new inner authority I'd never had before. I had been such a people-pleaser up until this point in my life and now all of that was changing. So in the process, I started to express more of who I really was, and even though I had wonderful bosses and great jobs, I realised I wasn't able to fully express the 'me' that I was becoming. So it was a time of real evolution. By about the third year of being at the school, I found myself more and more interested in facilitating this healing

> 66 Deepak Chopra has been another major influence in my life. 99

modality for others as a profession. From that point onward, I started to plan my homecoming. I felt a strong calling to bring this work back home to Queensland. By this stage I was living in California and although I loved it, it didn't feel right to stay on there. Plus, I knew I had more unfinished pieces of my own self-healing that could only happen once I stepped back onto home soil.

What attracted you to the area of healing?

First and foremost, it was for me. There were areas of my life that weren't working, and I had unresolved issues. When I ran off and joined DFAT at age 21, it really was like an escape. My home life as a child and adolescent had been quite turbulent, full of highs and lows. So I created this colourful life as a bit of a camouflage to hide behind. If I'd stayed in Brisbane I probably would have learnt the same lessons I needed to learn but I guess I just chose a more vibrant backdrop against which to play them out. And given the chance again, I wouldn't change a thing! Even before I went on to study healing, I experienced it through absorbing the world's beauty. My first years in Europe were profound in this respect. Before the UN days, I had a posting at our embassy in Vienna and it was during this time that I soaked up music and art like a sponge. At least two or three nights every week I was at either the opera or some magnificent palace for a concert or cultural event. Just walking those cobblestoned streets was a feast of art in itself. And this is where I first began to really heal at those deep inner levels. This is the message I feel I want to bring as my gift to the planet: that we heal through beauty, not through struggle; we heal through pleasure, not through repression.

What studies have you done to assist the healing work that you do?

I completed a Diploma in Brennan Healing Science, which is a four-year program. The training was structured whereby you attended five separate residential training weeks every year for four years. In between those residential weeks, there was a high volume of practical application, reading and written assignments. So the assessment process really was continuous. At the same time we were required to be in full-time psychotherapy because of the accelerated transformation process. The Barbara Brennan School of Healing moved from New York to Miami, Florida, in my final year of the training because the Florida Board of Education recognised the school as a tertiary institution. Students can now graduate with a Bachelor of Science, which I think adds further credibility to the profession.

I've also trained as a practitioner in Neuro-Linguistic Programming (NLP) and have a Certificate in Time-Line Therapy. These are wonderful tools for tapping into the unconscious mind to clear negative behavioural patterns, to get to the source of an issue and then to create new positive outcomes. NLP is also a great technique for understanding the different languages that we all speak. Some people are very visual and others are more auditory or kinaesthetic. When we can connect with the particular language of 'the other', there is an enhanced level of understanding and depth of contact.

Deepak Chopra has been another major influence in my life. He was my first introduction to quantum physics and how we create our own reality through where we focus our attention. I did his Synchro-Destiny course, which was all about harnessing the power of coincidence and synchronistic events as a way of charting our own destiny and manifesting our intentions.

You define yourself as a 'Wholistic Life Coach'. What does this mean?

My own definition of a 'Wholistic Life Coach' is someone who:

- explores with their client their goals and desires
- encourages and supports them to live life to their fullest potential
- mirrors back to the client their inner beauty and 'core essence'
- facilitates energy healing techniques to enhance the manifestation process, thereby integrating spiritual purpose with earthly reality.

How do you help your clients?

I think that what I provide for my clients is first:

- *A safe container* – a space where they can fully express themselves and take time out for them.
- *A listening ear* – an opportunity for them to articulate aspects of their lives that might be troubling them and what they want to change.

Then I love exploring with my clients the deeper layers of what might be blocking them from living their life the way they would like to. Talking things through is immensely valuable, but it's only part of the process. This is where the energy work takes over and enables real transformation to occur. When energetic debris is cleared from a person's energy field, it's like removing the fog that blocks the sun. Their innate essence can then shine through more strongly, and their sense of purpose can strengthen. Last but not least, the client receives an energetic 'alignment' with their goals and intentions. It's like a 'seeding' process and this is where magic starts to happen. Everyone's path is different, everyone's timing and rhythm is different. Some people create positive change for themselves very swiftly, whereas for others it's a more gradual process. There is no right or wrong way – everyone's journey is sacred and right for them.

What type of clients do you have and why do you consult with you?

I have clients from all walks of life, from the so-called 'alternative' types right through to very 'mainstream' people. In my experience, most people are searching for something, whether it's physical or emotional wellbeing, a desire to feel more connected with their spiritual self, or a deeper sense of meaning or purpose in their life. I find that pretty much everybody wants to achieve some kind of greater fulfilment, no matter who they are and what they do. We're like nature itself. We all go through cycles of growing, expanding, flowering, shedding, contracting, balancing, then growing and expanding some more. A lot of people come to me when they're in the midst of change or at a crossroads. This can be the time people need the most support.

Do you believe it is possible for people to heal themselves?

Absolutely! We are all spiritual beings having a human experience on planet Earth, so we all come fully equipped with an in-built self-healing mechanism. We see this in every day examples – someone cuts their finger and within a few days it has healed again. The same theory can be applied to any illness or ailment. We have the same capacity to heal anything. Our cells are constantly renewing themselves, which means that with conscious awareness we can reverse any disorder or disease. When a problem manifests itself at the physical level, that's the final wake-up call. It means that we haven't caught it at the psychological or emotional level first. There is always an emotional and psychological component behind every physical ailment.

66 There is no right or wrong way – everyone's journey is sacred and right for them. 99

We are multidimensional beings and at the core of ourselves we carry a spark of the divine. We are powerful co-creators. It's through life's twists and turns, and the duality of living on the Earth plane, that we forget the truth of who we really are and we begin to believe in a more distorted reality. These distortions can be corrected, and often it takes an illness for some people to slow down long enough to allow the reversal process to take place.

So in the work that I do, we're dealing with the fact that energy equals consciousness, and consciousness equals energy. When someone has a shift in awareness, one of those 'ah ha' moments, there is a shift in their energy field, which can then impact positively at the physical level.

You believe that people are afraid to 'want what they want'. What does this mean?

I think there can be a fear of failure that causes people to become paralysed and unable to take action. First, some people are afraid to become powerful because they had a negative role model in their lives, where power was destructive or abusive in some way. This can set up an unconscious belief system that to be powerful is wrong, dangerous or bad. I work with this theme quite a bit. Then there's the other side of the coin where the fear of success can paralyse people. This is especially true if they've observed other successful people being chopped down, criticised or losing friends or family. So often the solution for these people is to shove all of those desires and dreams back inside and to stay 'safe'. I'm not saying it's always like this, but I witness these dilemmas often.

When we talk about our 'shadow' selves, most people would think of the 'dark shadow' of our personality or some negative aspect. But we also have a 'golden shadow', where we can be almost terrified of seeing our own brilliance. Marianne Williamson once said, 'Our deepest fear is not that we are inadequate...but that we are powerful beyond measure'. However, she also says, 'As we are liberated from our own fear, our presence automatically liberates others'. So I think this is a very encouraging concept and one I believe to be true. This is something I'm very passionate about in my work with people. I love coaxing others out of those fearful places, both verbally and energetically, and encouraging them to 'want what they really want'. It's such a celebration when that inner light starts to come forth and a whole new sense of freedom emerges, like unlocking the door of our own self-imposed prisons!

Is there a significant quote or saying which you live your life by?

I love a poem called *The Journey* by Mary Oliver. It speaks about those times in our lives, the major crossroads, where we just know that change is inevitable. As excruciating as that might be, both for ourselves and others, we realise we no longer have a choice. It's as if our own destiny has made the choice for us. The poem is about listening to that inner voice, the voice of our soul. It concludes with the words, 'Determined to save the only life that you could save'. I'm so grateful that this poem exists because it has helped me make sense of the crossroads in my own life.

The other poem that strongly resonates with me is *Love after Love* by Derek Walcott. He paints a vivid picture of coming back home to self. The words have been such a source of comfort for me during the times when I felt really lost, when I felt trapped by circumstances and wondered 'What's it all about? What am I really doing here?' This poem has helped me put it all back into perspective. The last line of the poem is, 'Sit. Feast on your life'. It's a poem of real healing.

And a quote of my own is 'Beauty heals'. I am extremely passionate about those two little words. Beauty and pleasure are incredible healing forces, whether it's through nature, the ocean, art, music, some kind of aesthetic design, or a fabulous meal. It's going to be different for everyone, but these are just some of the things that do it for me and as a result, 'Beauty Heals' has become my life's motto!

What are the common threads of successful people you have met around the world?

* fearlessness
* determination

- focus
- being true to their own beliefs
- generosity
- passion
- humility.

What are some of your goals for the next five years?

I'd love to become a motivational speaker on a bigger scale in order to really encourage people to 'want what they want' and believe they can have it. Whenever I've done seminars, workshops or radio interviews, I've loved that sense of contact one gets from a larger audience – there's something really exhilarating about it. I'd also like to do some work again with the UN, this time in my current capacity as a 'Wholistic life coach'. It's a huge bureaucracy and a bit of a tough nut to crack, but they have begun to focus on wellness programs for staff, especially with so many peacekeeping missions around the world. I made one attempt a couple of years ago, so it's probably time to give it another go.

Another goal I have is to spend part of my time as a travel writer – to go on assignment to beautiful destinations and critique some stunning resort or new boutique hotel. New horizons at regular intervals are what feed my soul. I also plan to write my own book, expanding on my journey so far and how I believe we can heal ourselves.

What do you love most about being where you are today?

Being my own boss. It's been the most liberating experience of my life. It was a major step for me to take, after being in such structured organisations up until that point, but again it was one of those choices that was no longer a choice – it was the next obvious step.

Did you ever have to choose between love and your career?

Even though I became a bit of a moving target for 20 years, I didn't miss out on love! I'm a Taurean, born in the Year of the Pig, so love is fundamental to me! There are ways of adjusting your career to fit love in and ways of adjusting love to fit your career in. It probably meant a few more plane trips and bigger phone bills at times. Okay, I haven't done the white dress and the babies thing, nor the picket fence in the suburbs thing either, but I somehow knew that was not my path anyway. And now a whole new chapter is here…new beginnings. I feel like the best years of my life are still ahead of me. And maybe it's still not too late for the white dress!

At the end of your life how do you want to be remembered?

In the end I want to be remembered as someone who lived her life to the full, someone who overcame her fears and inhibitions and went on to fulfil her mission and purpose. That mission is to let others know that they too can heal their wounds by discovering their passion, by finding what represents beauty and pleasure in their own life, and letting all that come forth to transform their world and the world of those around them.

FREE BONUS GIFT

Miriam Schafer has kindly offered a FREE BONUS GIFT valued at $14.95 to all readers of this book...

A Collection of Inspirational Quotes – Miriam has been an avid collector of quotes for most of her life. In this wonderful e-book she has compiled some of the most heart-warming quotes written by the world's most gifted writers. Guaranteed to uplift your spirit, the wisdom they contain will inspire new thoughts and light the path to greater happiness and fulfilment.

Simply visit the private web page below and follow the directions to download direct to your Notebook or PC.

www.SecretsExposed.com.au/inspiring-women

JO COWLING

66 The show has had a positive affect on my professional life because now that I have much better health, not only physically but also mentally, pressure is like water off a duck's back! 99

JO COWLING

Jo Cowling was born in Kuala Lumpur, Malaysia, where her Australian father was a professional golfer. She moved to Australia at six months of age and spent her formative years growing up in Newcastle, New South Wales.

Jo works as a real estate agent on Sydney's Northern Beaches, but is probably best known as a contestant on the television show *The Biggest Loser*. Based on her positive nature and passion for life, Jo was selected for the show which saw her lose a staggering 31 kilograms – almost 30 per cent of her body weight – in a mere four months. This experience has since helped Jo recognise the importance of balance and placing an equivalent value on good physical and mental health. She has been an inspiration to many people and hopes to continue helping others when they too are ready to take the journey.

Since leaving the show, Jo continues to exercise daily and loves her sessions with her trainer Rod Collins, who she claims is responsible for helping her lose the majority of her weight outside *The Biggest Loser*. Jo accepts that this is the life she should have started living many years ago, and while she has no regrets she is certainly making up for lost time as she continues to wring each and every drop out of life!

What do you think has been the secret to your success?

Passion, persistence and drive have been the secrets to my success, plus surrounding myself with like-minded positive people who enhance me. I also think that understanding and appreciating that at times things get hard, but it doesn't mean that you give up. You simply need to learn to rise to the occasion and understand that each new experience is a learning curve that sets you up for future challenges. And without doubt, honesty is always the best policy – it takes years to build up a good reputation and you could easily shatter it within seconds if you take short cuts.

How would you describe yourself as a person?

Loyal, passionate, driven, dedicated, fun, caring, loving, a little crazy, quirky and unique. I like to see myself as a glass half-full kind of gal.

What has been the greatest moment in your life so far and why?

Each day in life is a momentous achievement, as I like to literally wring each and every drop out of life that I can. But if I had to pinpoint something I would have to say losing over 31 kilograms in 12 weeks on *The Biggest Loser* and being fit and fabulous!

Have you always had a problem with your weight, and if so, how did this affect you growing up?

I was always one of the 'bigger girls' throughout late primary school and the first half of high school but I was also one of the tallest. Once my growth spurt finished everyone else around me caught up, and some continued past me! I really stacked on the kilograms when I moved to Sydney some ten years ago. I lived a very sociable lifestyle with no exercise and a passion for fine dining! Personally, I've never had an issue with my weight – I was me and you either took me as I was or you didn't

> 66 I was over 115 kilograms, which is massive for a 165 centimetre frame. 99

take me at all. Mum was always on my back though, but it's only now that I realise it was for my health and not my appearance.

My weight didn't hold me back from doing things and I was always an active participant in sports. I suppose when it came to fashion I had to look around harder for things to suit me. I was 'bigger' but it was not until I hit my early twenties that I started to become severely overweight and then obese. I lived by the adage 'work hard, play hard' and the weight soon stacked on – at my heaviest, before being diagnosed with PCOS (Polycystic Ovarian Syndrome), I was over 115 kilograms, which is massive for a 165 centimetre frame. My social life revolved around good times and food – exercise was not high on my priorities in my twenties when really it should have been at the top of the list. At times I am positive that strangers were probably saying things about my weight behind my back, but because such loving and caring people have always surrounded me I didn't notice. Perhaps I chose to put my head in the sand! Since losing the weight one of the best compliments I have ever received is 'Joey, I didn't realise that you were so big. I just saw you for you'.

What made you decide to go on *The Biggest Loser*?

I applied for *The Biggest Loser* because my specialist, who treats me for PCOS, advised me that I was going to become an insulin-dependent diabetic if I didn't do something about my weight within six months. I am so scared of needles that I knew I could not face this path. I saw the advertisement on television one night and applied the next day. I saw *The Biggest Loser* as a lifeline to getting fit and healthy. I knew that if I had to stand up in front of the nation and admit that I had a problem then there would be no turning back. I have always been very good at being accountable to others and I am always reliable, but when it came to *me* I was forever avoiding the issue of my weight. Enough was enough and I knew that I had to do something before it was too late. *The Biggest Loser* was my last chance for getting my act together – everything else in my life was perfect and complete except the most important thing, my health and fitness!

When you were accepted, what was the first thing that went through your mind?

Fear. Excitement. I was about to embark on the most life-changing journey, so obviously a whole gamut of emotions and questions were running through my mind. Would I be able to succeed? What would other people think when they saw my overweight body in all its glory? Did I care that everyone in the nation would know how much I weighed? Would I like the other people I had to live with? I was definitely scared, but excited as well. I was being given an opportunity that money could not buy. With over 6,000 applicants, I was one of the fortunate 12 who were going to be given an amazing kick-start to a new life.

What were some of your goals when you started *The Biggest Loser*?

I am actually the world's worst goal setter. I think I do make them but don't realise that I do. I understand the importance of goal setting and want to be more aware of setting them. During the filming of the show, my only goal was to 'stay alive!' I am reading a lot of books at the moment to help with my self-development and many are focusing on goal setting – this is my next big challenge.

Can you describe what a typical day was like for you when you were on the program?

A typical day? With producers constantly springing surprises on us, the day could involve anything. However, usually we would wake up around

5am and get prepared for the day. We were not allowed out into the grounds until the house manager opened the doors. Preparing breakfast involved recording calories in our diaries for our trainers and dieticians. I must admit that many hours of the day were often spent in transit, as the producers would often send us to specific venues for filming, especially for the challenges. We really only ever saw the trainers for around one-and-a-half hours a day, five days a week. The balance of the two-and-a-half hours of training was basically up to us and I preferred going out and training within the grounds rather than indoors (I have always been a free spirit like that). Filming took up the best part of the day so we were often exhausted by dinner. With more training to fit in we often didn't make it into bed until 11pm before having to get up, bones aching, to do it all over again.

When you eventually left the show, what made you keep up your weight loss?

I knew that there was no turning back and I wanted to succeed. I found myself a fabulous trainer, Rod Collins, who owns Focus Health Training at Warriewood Beach and immediately clicked with him. Rod got into my head and helped me on my journey. I credit him for the bulk of my success as the majority of the weight I lost was after I left the house. Rod would train me for three hours a day, for five, sometimes six, days a week. He and his partner, Sally, are absolute gems who genuinely care and this is so important. I also train with an amazing group of people who have been training together for over six years. They welcomed me into their 'A-Team' fold with open arms, which I appreciated. They keep my spirits high and I get to laugh heaps while burning 1,500 calories a session – perfect!

After I left the show, I started to trust my body and believe in its strength – it was a buzz to watch my weight drop and my resting heart rate reached an all-time low. It was also amazing to feel myself get stronger, not only physically but also emotionally – this was very empowering and it certainly kept me motivated.

What does your workout/diet schedule involve now that you are finished with the show?

I now train four to five times a week. I still train with Rod three times a week doing outdoor training with a small group which involves running, playing an array of ball games, working out on the beach, running up steps, and lots of other fun things for around an hour, followed by 30 minutes of weights. I was recently given a membership to a 'conventional' gym, so I do some classes there, but I really enjoy my outdoor sessions!

When it comes to diet, my theory is to not deprive myself. If I want something I have it – I just need to factor in the calories. If I want to go out somewhere special for dinner, I simply eat fewer calories during the day and train a little harder. It all seems to be working so far and I feel more balanced. I am living a lifestyle now, not dieting. No more dieting for me!

What have been some of the best food tips you have learnt in terms of healthy eating?

People often think that when you want to lose weight you need to starve yourself. This is so untrue! The fact of the matter is that yes, you need to reduce your calories, but you also need to be filling yourself up with good fuel such as fresh vegetables, lean meats and fish, and in small amounts good carbs, and fats such as almonds.

The best way to lose weight is to eat five or six small meals a day to ensure that you are giving your body the energy it needs to function. I've found that organic oats with some nuts and seeds mixed with low-fat yoghurt is a great kick-start for the day. Morning and afternoon tea might be something like a couple of Vita Weets with low-fat cheese or a small handful of

66 Filming took up the best part of the day so we were often exhausted by dinner. 99

nuts, and I tend to have a larger lunch if I am going to be training in the afternoon. I've found that chicken breast, grilled fish and lean roasted meats with salads give me good energy and a sense of feeling full.

If I want a 'treat' I might have a kebab and only eat half of it. My favourite is lean chicken with loads of salads, no cheese and extra hot chilli sauce to get the metabolism going! You need to treat yourself.

Basically though, if it hasn't had any 'human intervention' (that is, it's natural and hasn't been processed) it's almost always good for you!

It must have taken a lot of motivation and self-control to continue. What top five tips would you give to other women who are looking to lose weight?

1. Lose weight for yourself – nobody else!
2. Rid yourself of people who are negative in your life.
3. Find something that you enjoy doing – don't feel that you need to join a gym. Walk the dog, shop, swim, dance.
4. If you fall off the horse don't be hard on yourself – tomorrow is another day. Learn to forgive yourself.
5. Learn to say 'no'. If you don't want to do something don't do it – focus on you and your needs always.

What have you gained from being on *The Biggest Loser* and what was the most important lesson you learnt?

My newfound health has been the best thing to come out of *The Biggest Loser*. It's amazing how you can punish your body for so many years but when you give it some tender loving care it begins to fire on all pistons again. I have so much energy, I love it. I'm also a born shopper, so it's really cool to be able to walk into a shop and try on any outfit (and it fits!). I have learnt that you really need to look deep within yourself to work out what makes you happy. Once you are happy within yourself, everything else seems to fall into place.

Before *The Biggest Loser.*

Jo at her final weigh-in.

Do you have any regrets about going on the show? If so, what are they?

66 Regrets are not worth the energy that you expend on them... 99

I have had no regrets about going on the show, although I often have moments where I wish I could have my anonymity back. The pressures of the media can be gruelling, but it's a small price to pay to add 30 years to my life! Live, love and enjoy! Regrets are not worth the energy that you expend on them – having fun is far more advantageous!

How authentic is the 'reality' aspect of reality television?

The short answer is that there are snippets of reality – any reality television show is based on real content that has happened during the filming. I believe that the reality is minimised during the editing and cutting process, when the producers are trying to portray a particular angle. I thought that when I went on *The Biggest Loser* we would just be followed around by a camera crew as we slogged away like mice on a treadmill. But the majority of the time was spent being transported to locations and re-shooting scenes from several different angles.

It was quite daunting to watch the pieces that went to air. While some came across as they happened, other scenes were given a particular slant to emphasise a point or to 'tell a story'. This was initially quite difficult to accept as we were really the only people that knew what was truly happening. I have had to learn to have broad shoulders as some people, particularly those on internet forums, were basing their judgements on us solely from what they had seen on television. During times like these I was lucky to have good, loving and supportive people around me.

How has being on *The Biggest Loser* affected your professional life?

I am extremely lucky that I have a very supportive boss who rode the emotional roller-coaster with me. I actually changed roles within our company after the show to focus further on marketing rather than selling, as I felt that I needed a change. If anything, the show has had a positive affect on my professional life because now that I have much better health, not only physically but also mentally, pressure is like water off a duck's back!

How hard is it to balance weight loss and work a job in real estate?

I used to think that finding a balance would be hard, but in fact all you have to do is diarise your exercise time and stick to it. I've found that by committing to an exercise routine I have a clearer mind and can function better at work. Just like anything you want to do in life, it requires commitment. We are so often making commitments to other people that we forget to make commitments to ourselves – the most important person in the equation!

There must be days when you have thought that it's all too hard and you've had enough. What gets you through the tough times?

Tough times are merely obstacles set to challenge you to think outside the square. When something comes up you just have to learn to deal with it. Nine times out of ten, people create far more drama in their lives then necessary. Once they decide to 'let go' they will find that they hardly have any challenges whatsoever.

How important has it been to surround yourself with people that believe in you and want to help you succeed?

Very important! You need a good strong support network of people who love you for you and want you to get the most out of everything you do. Don't surround yourself with doubting Nellies or people who don't want you to rise to the challenge because they will then feel inferior. The care and love of friends and family is a great motivator, but don't forget the journey begins from within.

If there was one thing you could say to women who feel that the chance for them to lose weight has passed, what would it be?

The clock has not stopped. It is never too late. Get moving now and you will thank yourself for it! As women we are powerful and strong – my goodness, if we can give birth to children we can do anything!

Do people need to attend a gym to lose weight?

Not at all! I don't think it matters where you do it, as long as you develop the desire to do so. Going for a walk outdoors is far more inspiring to me then being stuck in a gym running on a treadmill. I need the stimulation of fresh air and scenery to really get me into the moment. Better still, exercising outdoors is free. You can also work on your strength training by doing push-ups and squats in the park and by purchasing some hand-weights that you can use. You don't need to commit to a gym membership to get healthy, you just need to commit to getting active!

What would you say to women who think they just don't have enough time in the day to start exercising?

When are you planning on dying? Take time out to spend on yourself. If you have time for a facial or a pedicure, you have time to take a 30-minute walk each day. There are enough hours in a day, you just need to plan them. Stop making excuses because the longer you procrastinate the more time you lose on your life. Once you start exercising you will find that you actually enjoy it. I never believed this could be true for me before I started training but it is the adrenaline high which is the most amazing thing that you could ever experience.

What do you think are the essential qualities or personal attributes of a successful person?

I believe that honesty has to come first, if you can't tell the truth you have nothing. Following this is the need to be caring, considerate and willing to go that extra mile. I have also learnt that it is important to only take on projects where you can commit your heart and soul 100 per cent. Without the passion for something you will never have the drive or ambition to be your best. It's okay to say 'no' if you don't think something is right for you.

Who are the role models or mentors that have inspired you? What important lessons have you learnt from them?

Mum is so inspiring to me. She left her birth country over 33 years ago to follow her heart after meeting Dad, who was working as a professional golfer in Malaysia. She left a privileged life to come to a new country with barely any English and without a support network. It wasn't until my dad passed away almost 20 years ago that I truly appreciated the extent of my mum's strength – she is a special woman who always cares for others.

Another role model is my boss, Lachlan Elder. I have worked with Lachlan for ten years and he continually amazes me. He is a leader in his field and an extremely dynamic and charismatic person who understands the importance of balance

66 Once you start exercising you will find that you actually enjoy it. 99

in life. He is a great boss and extremely generous, with both his time and money.

How does it feel when people call you a role model and tell you that you have inspired them?

I actually still find this very bizarre. I don't see myself as anything special. If anything I am disappointed in myself that I didn't do something sooner to get fit and healthy. I have always been a passionate, positive, confident person with everything that I have ever undertaken in my personal and professional life, with the exception of my weight. It is easy for me to say 'If only I had done something sooner', but that said, I have always lived a full life.

Twelve months on from the show people still stop me daily for a chat, and you know what? That inspires me to continue on my journey. These people inspire me and are my role models. It is so refreshing to know that they are prepared to come up to a total stranger and give them praise. I've had people come by my gym just to say hello and there was also a lovely lady named Roslyn, who emailed me after her workplace put together their own 'Biggest Loser' challenge. She was so sweet and lovely and I do hope that I have managed to assist her and motivate her, even if it's only in a small way. If I can help just one person, just as I have been helped, I will be very happy indeed!

If you had your time over again is there anything you would do differently?

Absolutely not! I have had a very blessed life. I am surrounded by great family, friends and colleagues and I have been very fortunate. There are times when I have lived by 'the law of accident' but I seem to be like a cat – somehow I just keep landing on my feet. I'm not sure how many of my nine lives I have used up now!

JENNIFER JEFFERIES

" The reality is that there are things in life that
we all need to do sometimes. So for me the way
that I can achieve the most out of my life is to
get the 'not so much fun' things done first and
then enjoy the rest. "

JENNIFER JEFFERIES

Jennifer Jefferies was born in Inala, a western suburb of Brisbane, in 1961. The second eldest of five children, Jennifer was always interested in pulling things apart to find out how they worked or how she could fix them.

At the age of 12 Jennifer decided that she wanted to join the Queensland Police Force as a cadet but found out that she was too short. At 15 she left school and worked in her family's service station until she was old enough to enlist in the Australian Army.

After three years' service, Jennifer resigned and worked in positions that called for 'street smarts', working her way up into management positions until finally she burnt out. At 28, she reinvented herself and studied natural therapies. She has since become one of Australia's best-known authors and speakers.

Today Jennifer speaks to corporations throughout Australia, Taiwan, China, Hong Kong, South Korea, the United States, Europe and New Zealand. She shares practical real-life strategies that help people to improve their health, wellbeing and productivity by finding balance in their lives. Jennifer is a refreshingly down-to-earth, engaging and informative speaker who leaves her audiences feeling empowered about the things they can do to achieve balance in their lives, rather than feeling guilty about what they're not doing!

Jennifer is the author of 7 Steps to Sanity® and seven other health-related titles which are sold throughout the world, having been translated into four languages. When Jennifer is not travelling she can be found hanging out with her partner, Toni, and their two cats on the Gold Coast, or riding her beloved motorbike with the guys and girls from the Gold Coast Cruiser Motor Bike Club.

Starting out what were some skills you were lacking and what did you do about it?

Growing up I was never inspired at school and was one of those kids who couldn't leave fast enough. I left when I was 15, so I never experienced senior education or university and to be honest, I never wanted it or missed it. I got out into the world, picked up real life skills and got a grounding that I could never have gotten from school at that time. I was fortunate that my employers saw early on that I was street smart and they were able to nurture that, allowing me to bring different qualities to the positions I held.

Since then I have studied and earned an assortment of qualifications, and I now know the benefit of constant study. I know that I will never stop learning, and I am always hungry for it, but I find that learning in a classroom is simply not my style. I like to learn at my own pace and am the kind of person that craves to be out there doing it, diving in headfirst and learning lessons along the way, not just learning about the theory of it.

How did your time in the Army impact your life?

The Army gave me an amazing grounding for life. Joining as an 18-year-old meant that I needed to grow up real fast. I was extremely naive when I joined, but the support and sense of community that you get in the services allowed me to grow and thrive. I was able to develop my sense of self within a team environment and with people who pushed me to be all that I could be. It can be a challenge to explain to someone who has not experienced it, but the comradeship and sense of community that you find in something like the services is very special. I received more life lessons in three years in the regular Army than most people get in a lifetime. Saying I loved those years would be an understatement – my time and adventures in the Army are among my most treasured memories so far.

> 66 I am very comfortable with my sexuality and understand the laws of attraction... 99

Given your sexuality, did you experience prejudices of any kind? If so, how did it affect you and what did you do about it?

When I was a young teenager I chose to live my life being true to myself. When I was 17 or 18 I started to understand that I was gay. I was still in the Army when I came out in 1979, and it was not necessarily a gay-friendly environment in those days. As I had made a conscious choice to never hide my sexuality I did initially attract some negative attention from the military police, but the commandant of my battalion was very supportive and provided that I did my job just like anyone else, he had no hassles with me. For me the negative attention had a reverse effect to what they probably wanted. It made me more determined to 'be me', to live a true life and never hide my sexuality or anything else about me.

Outside of the Army I have never really attracted any negative attention that I am aware of. I am very comfortable with my sexuality and understand the laws of attraction, so I don't attract negative experiences.

You later became involved in health in the corporate arena. What lessons did this teach you?

I learnt that everyone is human and we all go off track sometimes. As a naturopath, the thing we are challenged with is patient compliance, and I know from my work and research with busy 'corporates' that when they are stressed they still tend to reach for the extra cup of coffee first. Going to a bunch of busy corporates and telling them that they couldn't have their coffee was not going to achieve anything. Through my work I have become what I call a 'realistic naturopath'. I understand that people go off track, but I now give them the skills to come back guilt-free. So my biggest lesson was about allowing people to be individuals and accepting that they are very human, especially when under stress.

You were involved in a serious car accident. Why was this event such a major turning point in your life?

I had been riding the fun times of the eighties – playing in the corporate world and not necessarily caring about anything except making money and being successful. I was so off balance that I could no longer see what my life was really like. My car accident made me do two things. First, it made me realise how precious life is and how I had been taking it and everyone in it for granted. Second, it showed me how responsible I was for my own health, both physically and emotionally. Although the car accident made me sit up and listen, I could also see how easy it could have been to continue living the life that I was living prior to the accident. Changing the way you live your life can be a scary thing and I'm extremely glad that I was able to make that change.

At the height of your corporate career, you believe that you ignored the signals your body was sending you. In hindsight, what were those signals?

For about two years before I exited the corporate world I had been getting lots of little symptoms like broken sleep (I was waking tired and was slow to get going), headaches, and a tight neck and shoulders. I was emotionally flat, tired and cranky, my digestive system was all over the place, I needed a glass or two of alcohol to wind down at night, and I was propping myself up with stimulants like caffeine and sugar. The scary thing is that on some strange level I thought that was normal and justified it as being okay because I was working hard to be successful. The reality was that my body was telling me to slow down and was giving me symptoms to make me do it. When I take a step back, it's easy to see that there were distinct signs, but I was so 'in it' that I could not see what was really going on. That is why I am so focused today on teaching others what to look out for and how to live a life of prevention to avoid burning out.

In your opinion what impact does stress have on the body and mind?

The main body systems responsible for our ability to cope with stress are the adrenal glands. These are small triangular organs that sit like caps on top of each kidney and provide us with the surge of adrenaline that we need when we are faced with situations that call for unusual levels of physical or emotional exertion. The adrenals work a bit like a bank account – you spend a little adrenal energy each day and each night you build up your reserves again. But the reality is that most people spend more than they reinvest. In my work as a naturopath I found that almost all of my clients, regardless of what other physical ailments they had, were also experiencing adrenal fatigue or exhaustion.

The surge of adrenaline that we experience when we are under physical or emotional stress is called the 'fight or flight' response. Our heart rate increases, our blood pressure rises, our breathing becomes shallow and fast, and blood is diverted from our digestive system and other organs to our muscles so that we can stand and fight, or get the heck out of there. This was very useful in primitive times when we had to catch and kill our meals. Imagine being confronted by a wild creature and having to fight for your life or run for it – this is where the adrenals would kick in to give you the high-level burst of mental alertness and physical strength to help you survive. In these situations we had the opportunity to expel the adrenal energy by 'fighting or fleeing', the stress response would soon subside and life would return to normal. Today, people are fighting different types of battles on a daily basis that, although they are not necessarily life and death situations, can feel just as stressful. The difference is that we are not expelling our adrenal energy through 'fight or flight', and the stressful situations we experience are relentless, so we are not getting the chance to properly recharge our adrenals.

The adrenals can adapt and handle stress for extended periods of time, which makes people think that they are coping, when in fact their bodies are sitting on the edge of burnout. The way we adapt to ongoing stress is through a three-stage process called the 'General Adaptation

Syndrome'. The first stage is the 'alarm reaction' which is largely what I have just described as the 'fight or flight' response. The second stage is 'resistance'. This is where the adrenal glands adapt by increasing their size and function, but if extreme stress is maintained for a prolonged period the adrenals become tired, which causes them to under-function. If the stress is too extreme or continues for too long, the adrenals eventually lose their ability to recover. The final stage is 'exhaustion'. In this stage adrenal function is limited and the body has lost its ability to resist or cope with ongoing stress. This is when your adrenal bank account is empty and you are facing daily challenges to your health.

Some of the telltale signs of adrenal exhaustion include: frequent colds and flu, weakness, dark circles under the eyes, constant tension in the shoulders, specific markings on the iris (that can be identified through iridology), accelerated ageing and that persistent feeling of being 'burnt-out'. It can also manifest as a variety of ailments including headaches, backaches, insomnia, cramps, high blood pressure, chronic fatigue, reoccurring bacterial or viral infections and loss of libido. Among women, hormonal imbalances, menstrual irregularities, PMS, fibroids, endometriosis and fertility problems are also common.

What are your '7 Steps to Sanity®'?

The 7 Steps to Sanity® are for anyone that wants to have it all without losing their health, sense of humour or sanity along the way. The steps look at your physical and emotional health and give you practical tools to use in your everyday life to avoid adrenal burnout and stay sane. I find that most corporates appreciate the fact that while the 7 Steps to Sanity® are a stretch, they are also achievable and will help them to access more success and happiness in all areas of their lives. These are the steps that I followed in order to get myself

66 I was emotionally flat, tired and cranky, my digestive system was all over the place... 99

well and back on track after my car accident. It is also the system that I have used in my clinic for the past 15 years to help others get back and stay on track.

You have an interesting opinion about fear, can you share that with us?

Think about how your body responds when you are scared or sitting on the edge of stress. Your heart starts to race, you breathe shallow and fast, your gut knots up and your body gives you the ability to either stand and fight or get the heck out of there. Now think about how your body responds when you are really excited, your heart starts to race, but you breathe deeper. It is the breathing that takes you to a different place in the experience. One of the most useful tools you can have in life is to remember to breathe deeply. When you are in a stressful situation, just stopping for a moment and taking a deep breath allows you to see what is really happening, compared to what you think is happening.

From my experience any scary situation can be changed into an exciting one by taking a minute to stop, breathe and turn your focus around. Yes, I have been in some really 'exciting' situations in life, as we all have. The difference is that I was not exhausted and emotionally drained at the end of it. We cannot necessarily change the situations we are in, but we can change our perception of them and enjoy life again.

Why is it so important for people to learn to say 'no'?

Most of us are our own worst enemies when it comes to saying 'yes' to everything that is asked of us. I can't tell you the number of people that I have treated over the years who felt overloaded, fatigued and resentful for having been put in situations where they've had to do things that they either didn't want to do or didn't have time to do. The reality is that you create this situation by saying 'yes' when you should have said 'no'. You choose to forgo your own needs rather than having the courage to say 'no'. You choose to accept being overloaded rather than risk being thought of as selfish or inconsiderate. But have you ever thought about how unfair it is to say 'yes' to someone and then feel angry at them for it? If you are going to say 'yes', you need to mean it, get your head around it and get on with it. If you are saying 'yes' but meaning 'no' then you are heading into trouble.

There are enough stressors in life without creating new ones for yourself every time you are too afraid to say 'no'. No one likes to disappoint or let anyone down, but in life it's a reality – the only question is whether you will choose to always let yourself down by never letting anyone else down. It's time to show some respect for yourself and to start saying 'no'. It doesn't mean that you are selfish or don't care. It demonstrates that you understand your limits and are realistic about what can be achieved given your time, resources and capabilities. Respectfully saying 'no' shows others that you are not willing to disappoint their expectations by promising more than you can give.

> 66 Occasionally some things don't go quite to plan but I don't let that put me off... 99

We also have to learn to say 'no' to ourselves when we're not acting in our own best interests. You might have experienced the 'I'll just finish this one thing' syndrome, where you become so single-minded about your work that you neglect to look after the other areas of your life. It usually strikes after 5pm on a weekday and every time you think, 'I'll just finish this one thing' another hour slides by with you still sitting at your desk – then you grab something fast and fattening to eat, decide it's too late to go to the gym or that you're too tired to catch up with friends as planned and the 'poor me' behaviours begin to creep in. Negative emotions like 'poor me' suck the life out of you. It is generally unnecessary fear that stops us saying 'no'.

What steps did you take to get to where you are now?

I don't think I am your traditional businessperson in that I know I am supposed to have my goals written down and so forth. For me, I don't want to restrict the ideas my mind is playing with, so I have a loose plan with goals and I very much let it develop where it needs to go. That way I can still stay fluid enough to take advantage of any opportunities. Besides that, my mind never stops dreaming and it is constantly excited and thinking of what else is possible (which I have to admit challenges some of the people around me sometimes, but I love it). When I have a dream in mind I then look at it on a practical and realistic level, maybe bounce it off some friends and if I still have the excitement I jump in and give it a go. Occasionally some things don't go quite to plan but I don't let that put me off, it may just mean the idea needs a tweak.

Were there any times that you wanted to give up? What got you through?

Like every entrepreneur and business owner there have been times when I have seriously wanted to walk away from it all and go back to the perceived security of working for someone else and doing the nine-to-five job. The thing that stops me returning to that security is that when I initially stepped away from that life many years ago I realised that my life and potential for growth is limitless. Without the boundaries and restrictions of working for someone else I can take my business and life anywhere that I want to. To live a limitless life excites me beyond anything else, and for me to work with restrictions is not an option. Living a limitless life and coming from a belief of trust is what gets me through the challenging times.

You are a big promoter of the benefits of aromatherapy. Why do you believe it makes such a difference?

Through my own experiences and working with many patients over 15 years I know that negative emotions play a huge part in illness. Aromatherapy is about working with pure essential oils that are powerful natural compounds. The reason I like aromatherapy is that it is the easiest modality to integrate into all areas of your life and it can address physical and emotional imbalances in the body. You can take an aromatic bath or vaporise oils after a hard day at work, or switch your mind off to help you sleep at night, or re-energise yourself after a big night; it is a modality that even the layperson can gain benefit from.

Can you tell us why healthy eating isn't about depriving yourself of the foods you love to eat?

In clinic I found the most effective way to get people to live a healthy lifestyle was to get them to eat healthy foods as close to nature as possible six days a week, and on the seventh day I let them play. So on the seventh day they can eat whatever they want, guilt-free and with great enjoyment. When you tell someone they cannot eat a particular food for the rest of their life, they will crave it more, and eat twice as much of it because emotion will drive their actions. So to me balanced nutrition is about being really good the majority of the time but recognising the importance of being able to enjoy indulgences.

You say that the new food pyramid is actually a square. Can you explain what you mean?

You've heard of the food pyramid, you might have even learnt about it at school, and you can certainly picture it, at least vaguely, showing you what you should be eating in greater and lesser amounts to stay healthy – eat more of the stuff at the bottom and less of the stuff at the top and you'll be right.

Carbohydrate	Good Fats
Fruit and Vegetables	Protein

Water

As a naturopath I use a slightly different food pyramid, in fact I see it as a square in which the foods that we should be consuming are surrounded by the number one element our bodies need – water. I base it on what I have learnt on my travels and from working with the traditional diets in many Asian and European countries, which contain unprocessed foods, eaten close to their natural state. In these countries lifestyle-related diseases such as obesity, heart disease, diabetes and cancers, which commonly afflict Westerners, have not been experienced at anywhere near the same levels. People eating traditional diets enjoy good health. My food square focuses on a 'close to nature' balance, but that does not mean you have to live on lettuce leaves and water. It is about good quality unprocessed or unrefined foods.

Who are the role models or mentors that have inspired you? What important lessons have you learnt from them?

I remember being about 12 years old and reading Shirley MacLaine's first book, *Don't Fall off the Mountain,* and I was instantly taken to a place where I could see that anything was possible. I wanted to be just like Shirley, trekking and working all over the world and doing good for the universe. Over the years as I worked my way through all of her books I came to admire her even more for being a person who lived true to herself. It did not matter what flack she knew she would receive for putting herself out there and showing the world her true self, warts and all – she still did it and it inspired me to live my life being true to myself and not worrying about what others thought of me.

The person who inspired me to go back to school as an adult was a colleague from the pharmacy industry. I was 23 and I had commented that I was interested in furthering my education and she showed me that as an adult I could go back to school and learn again. Before that I had never thought of myself as being 'clever' enough to go to university or study formally. Her comments and belief in me that day changed my outlook on life and what was possible. Nowadays I have a hunger to learn. I love reading autobiographies and books with a business influence, and I like to see how real people have achieved success in their lives. People like Howard Schultz from Starbucks, Sir Richard Branson of Virgin and Oprah Winfrey all inspire me and I see them as mentors. Winston Churchill said, 'Never, never, never give up' and this is the common theme that keeps me seeking what is possible in life. If you believe in it and apply yourself, you can make it happen.

What is the best thing about being an Australian?

I think that we are so blessed to live in a country like Australia. My career has allowed me to travel the world, and with

> 66 ...on the seventh day they can eat whatever they want, guilt-free... 99

every trip I return home realising how fortunate I am to live in a country where I can live a limitless life and get out and give anything a go. I love how this characteristic is instilled in our Australian culture – it's okay to give things a go!

Is there a significant quote or saying which you live your life by?

Since my car accident I live by the rule that *'If it's hard to do that's all the more reason to do it'*. After my car accident I realised that life is preciously short and I did not want to lie on my deathbed wondering 'what if'. I also understood that by nature I am very human and love to procrastinate the things that I don't find fun to do. The reality is that there are things in life that we all need to do sometimes. So for me the way that I can achieve the most out of my life is to get the 'not so much fun' things done first and then enjoy the rest.

What do you see as the biggest challenge facing young women today and what can we do about it?

I think the biggest challenge facing not just young women, but young people in general, is their constant focus on what they don't have and the consequent negativity that keeps them down. If you keep focusing on a life that you don't like, you will never get to where you really want to be. I think the most important thing to do is to surround yourself with positive people and get a mentor or a positive role model if you have trouble keeping focused. I see this as the biggest challenge facing young people and I would love to see more real life skills being taught to young men and women at a school level.

Where do you see yourself in 20 years' time? What is your ultimate dream?

My ultimate dream is to build an empire that allows me the freedom and funds to set up a philanthropic network through which I can help the women of the world who don't have the opportunity and access to formal education to 'be all that they want to be'. Furthermore, I would like to help train them in basic business and life skills so that they too can have a limitless life. So in 20 years' time I will be surrounded by amazing people who will love helping others to live a similar life.

What is the one key idea that you want people to take from your journey?

I would love to see people of all ages understand that life is limitless. Surround yourself with people and things that feed your energy (for me that involves reading autobiographies, business motivation, and health and fitness books) and keep you on track. Then let go of the energy suckers in your life (for example, people you don't enjoy being around and unhealthy foods). Life is too short not to enjoy it. Simple things, such as deep breathing, make it so easy to turn bad situations into exciting adventures. Sometimes I feel that the amount of excitement I have for life will make me burst. I only hope that I can help other people to share in that excitement and live fulfilling lives too!

FREE BONUS GIFT

Jennifer Jefferies has kindly offered a FREE BONUS GIFT valued at $49.50 to all readers of this book...

Everything You Always Wanted To Know About How To Get A Life – Life Balancing expert, Jennifer Jefferies has taught some of the world's leading corporations how to help their staff to 'get a life'. With her 7 Steps to Sanity®, Jennifer has a prescription for modern living. In this no-nonsense and no-guilt-trip e-book, Jennifer will help you incorporate these powerful strategies into your everyday life. So start reading today and lead a more balanced, energised and happy life.

Simply visit the private web page below and follow the directions to download direct to your Notebook or PC.

www.SecretsExposed.com.au/inspiring-women

Kim McGuinness

KIM MCGUINNESS

66 I think the secret to success is valuing your time, understanding your limitations and staying as stress-free as possible! Success is also about focusing on those projects that are truly worthwhile... There are a lot of time-wasters out there! 99

KIM MCGUINNESS

Kim McGuinness was born in Sydney in 1966 to Danish and Scottish parents. From an early age, Kim was involved in organising social functions and running businesses such as car washing, dog walking and many lemonade stands!

After leaving school in 1984, Kim studied a Bachelor of Business while working full-time in the area of accounting and credit management. After realising this career was not for her, she began to focus her attention on her more creative talents. She entered the field of market research during a two-year stint in the UK where she thrived on building a strong rapport with her clients and was recognised for her leadership qualities and innovative flair. Upon her return to Sydney, Kim completed a Diploma in Marketing Management and is currently studying a Bachelor of Applied Science, majoring in web design.

Kim launched her highly respected company, Centrum Events, in 1999. Over the past eight years she has successfully staged many events catering for between ten and 2,000 delegates, and engaged speakers ranging from the unsung heroes of the business world to the Prime Minister of Australia. Among her clients are many of Australia's leading companies and associations, including CCH Australia, St James Ethics Centre, Australian Business Limited, and many more.

Kim is most widely recognised as the founder of The Businesswomen's Breakfast Series, which began in March 1999. The Businesswomen's Breakfast Series is now a part of Network Central which Kim established in November 2004. Kim was a finalist in the Sydney Business Review's Businesswoman of the Year Award in 2003 and was nominated for the Telstra Businesswoman of the Year in 2004, 2005 and 2006.

Kim now lives on the North Shore of Sydney with her husband and two small children.

What were some of your early influences in life?

My father was a senior financial executive when I was growing up and he had me doing budgets for everything! I had a budget for my pocket money at the age of eight and a budget for each business I had – car washing, babysitting and dog walking. I don't know how successful I was with budgeting money after I left school but I certainly had the basics! Dad's systems taught me the concept of covering expenses before you show a profit and the importance of cash flow. Although I am not a classic accountant, and now employ one to help with this area of my business, I certainly know my way around a budget and understand figures well enough to know where my business is going at all times.

My Danish grandmother, Mormor, was another major influence throughout my childhood. Mormor had an ingenuity that amazed me. She always solved problems by looking outside the classic solution and also loved to make things and see things created from the ground up. My grandfather was a master craftsman with an incredible workshop at home. There were many times when my grandmother and I raided the workshop to make something! Her attitude was, 'If you can't find it, make it'.

You worked your way to management by motivating people. How exactly did you do this?

I've learnt a lot from my mother who was a senior executive within a pharmaceutical company for many years. Her method of management was very collaborative and never competitive. She was a master at building effective teams and encouraged and treasured her staff. Motivation within a team comes from all angles – not just the manager. When I was with a company I tried to learn other aspects of the business and in three instances shifted jobs within the company. Once I found where I wanted to be then I worked hard to encourage those around me to improve and refine our way of doing things. I am not very good at sitting still and liked the challenge of change! I don't make a great employee as I

> 66 Give them a smile and they are more than happy to smile back! 99

get bored way too easily, but when I had a good project to get my teeth stuck into I loved it!

Was it difficult adjusting to Australia after spending so much time abroad?

Quite the opposite in fact! My travels widened my view of the world and made me appreciate this beautiful country of ours. I love the diversity of Australia and we truly do live in a beautiful land. If anything, my experiences working in Europe fuelled my desire to be an entrepreneur. It was interesting to see how companies in other countries operated and how other people lived and went about their business. It was interesting to live in a large city such as London with so many people. I learnt what a difference a smile can make! People are squashed into the tube, rushing everywhere and live on top of each other. A smile and a kind word made all the difference sometimes! Don't get me wrong, Londoners certainly know how to let their hair down and have a laugh with friends, and are fantastic people – it just showed me that the people you see on the way to where you are heading are important too. Give them a smile and they are more than happy to smile back!

In the beginning what were some skills you were lacking and what did you do about it?

When Centrum Events started I was very lucky in that I had come from an environment of business assistance and advice, so I utilised my already existing networks for information and support about starting the business. My husband also runs a medium-sized business so he was enormously helpful. Regarding the networking events, I involved a couple of already existing networks that weren't running events to help achieve more publicity and raise funds while establishing *our* events. Two heads really are better than one in a lot of circumstances and strategic alliances can be very powerful.

These days you can just about outsource anything so any skills lacking are easily found. I also believe that everyone has greatness around them if they just look for it. People I work with are always amazed by how much expertise is within their own network when they actually think about it. I also believe in constant learning – mentoring, tertiary studies, short courses and so on. Also, don't be afraid to ask someone you know for advice or help. Usually they are more than happy to share their expertise. Even people who you don't know personally are more than happy to let you buy them a cup of coffee – I certainly did this a few times when I was starting out and still do!

Where did the idea come from to start Network Central?

The idea for Network Central came about when I gave birth to my second child. I was wearing many hats and trying to look after myself and my new baby at the same time. I figured there must be others in this situation. As a business owner, mother and part-time student, I spend a considerable amount of time and money belonging to various groups and organisations that relate to my different roles. It occurred to me that we tend to live life as though the various aspects of our lives can be compartmentalised and don't impact one another. What I wanted to do was to bring together a broader networking resource, one that recognises the many different roles and responsibilities that businesspeople have.

I was already running the Businesswomen's Breakfast Series and producing corporate events and conferences through Centrum Events. I knew I couldn't continue to run multi-day conferences with two small children but didn't want to give up the Businesswomen's Breakfast Series. So I took the breakfast and gave it a home within Network Central, which was an innovative way of looking at an employee or business owner as a whole person, and not just a workhorse.

Network Central has a lot of respect in the marketplace. How did you develop credibility as a brand?

I think our credibility has evolved over the many years of running the Businesswomen's Breakfast Series and through a lot of referrals. For Network Central I invested a lot of time in the look and feel of the brand and the workings of the website in order to provide a quality environment and respectable image. It is so important to support the vision for the business with a solid infrastructure and good systems. I also listen to my customers and seek feedback regularly. There really is no other way to run a service-based business – or any other business for that matter. Your perception of how your business is doing can sometimes be very skewed and a regular dose of reality is essential. The business plan must therefore be flexible enough to turn corners and change direction easily.

How has faith played an important part in developing your business?

Creating Network Central in the first place was a massive leap of faith! I think creating any new business is always a risk, but as long as you are true to the purpose of the business and do your research properly then the risk is minimised.

Also, in my business I have to plan and commit to 12 months of event dates at the beginning of each year. It can be very hard to sign-off when so many other things are going on and sometimes the faith wavers a little! I have to trust that the business provides a valuable service and that I am doing the right thing. I have to trust that guests will attend the breakfast and I have to trust that people will keep coming back. I am solid in my conviction that quality networking is important to everyone and through regular feedback I know that the breakfasts are valued. As in any business, if you value who you are, who your customers are and what you do, then business will always follow.

Were there any times when you wanted to give up? What got you through?

Yes, there have definitely been times when I have wanted to give up! Particularly when the kids are sick, work is piling up, the washing hasn't been done and there is a major event on the next day! I don't think there is a soul on this planet who hasn't wanted to chuck it all in and go live in some remote part of the world at some point! What got me through is reminding myself that I am working this way for a reason and that the kids are only preschoolers for a short time. This puts everything into perspective.

First I give myself time to breathe – go play with the kids or take them for a walk and a milkshake – just to get out of the stressed environment for half an hour. Then I complete, or allocate a time to deal with, one urgent thing that needs to be done and tick it off my list (I love lists!). After this I prioritise everything else and outsource what I can. When the dust has settled I write down three reasons for doing what I do and what inspires me, and three reasons for giving up and what I would do instead. The reasons 'for' always win.

You are very proactive in the upbringing of your children. Why is this so important to you?

People do what works for them and this works for me. I don't expect that everyone would be able to run their business from home as I have and whatever works for an individual is great for them. People say, 'Happy wife, happy life', and that is true to an extent! It also goes for mothers – if the mother is happy and fulfilled then she is always a better mother to her children. Everyone has off days here and there and that is perfectly normal. Sometimes these days serve as reminders to focus on the important things in life!

> 66 I also listen to my customers and seek feedback regularly. 99

I was lucky that I had the luxury of being able to plan for the birth of my kids and set my business up four years prior to their arrival. Network Central was born after the second child but the bones of the business were there already. I always wanted to be at home for my children and am lucky to have been able to achieve that. I have had a tough year as it has been difficult to do everything, but in order to be the stay-at-home-mum that I wanted to be, I had to decide what I would sacrifice. In my case I have sacrificed planned growth and have just kept the business running as it is. As the children grow and go to school, I know I will have more time to concentrate on the business and execute the plans that I have created while the kids are young.

What is your philosophy on work/life balance and does it really exist?

My entire business is about balance – the various areas of the network are designed to address each area in our busy lives. The idea for Network Central came about when I was actually in labour with my second child, Juliet, who was early and threw all my carefully laid out plans into chaos!

The best balancing trick for me is to be 100 per cent present in whatever I am doing without feeling guilty for the other things I am not doing. If I am with the children then I am with them 100 per cent without feeling guilty about the business. On the other hand if I am working, I arrange this around preschool and sleep times so that I can concentrate completely on what I am doing – this way I am a lot more focused and a million times more efficient. I am a full-time mother and have structured my business around my children. For example, when my son was a baby it was easy to work longer hours as all he did was sleep. As he got older and the second one came along I outsourced various aspects and scaled back projects to allow for more time with them. Next year my son will start primary school and Juliet will go to preschool two days a week so I will have more time again to increase my programs. This year has been about planning and tweaking programs to roll out the next year. In the pursuit of balance I have also learnt to say 'no!'

Playing with my kids or taking time out is not only therapeutic, it's grounding and helps me to realise what is truly valuable in my life. It also allows the mind to clear and to think – some of my best creative ideas have been in the cubbyhouse over a cup of pretend tea!

What specific things do you do to balance your marriage, children and career?

I do everything I can to keep them separated and treat each one as importantly as the other. I have a rule that I will not work when my husband is home, unless absolutely necessary, as that is family time. I structure my time so that I am not working more than two hours in any one day when the kids are awake, and even then I break it into one-hour blocks while the kids are occupied doing an activity. I have two nights per week to myself and get through the bulk of my workload during these times. I have set up systems to manage the business and have employed a company to staff the phones, take messages and make event bookings, which has made an incredible difference. We also employ a fabulous cleaner – the best investment ever made! I have outsourced the things I am not good at or don't like doing and this allows me to focus on the core business and the children. As I have more time I will do more with the business but for now this system works for me. A business should always be flexible and able to expand and contract when required without losing momentum. I am incredibly motivated by the business and the amazing people within the network so it is never a chore to pick it up and put it down.

I am also a big believer in not feeling guilty. I don't feel guilty for the business when I am in the backyard having a tea party with my daughter and I don't feel guilty for the hour when the kids are doing an activity and I am nearby working on my laptop. My children understand when Mummy is busy and it has taught them both patience and respect for

66 I am incredibly guilty of having all these grand ideas and taking on too much at once. 99

other people. They are also very good at un-stuffing nametags after events now! The kids also understand (usually!) when Mummy and Daddy are talking and allow us time to have a conversation – quite a rare thing when the kids are awake! We try to eat dinner as a family each night and catch up then. I believe in treasuring your friends and family and we try to do something social each week. Yes, this is all good in theory and sometimes everything goes haywire but, hey, that's life!

How important are boundaries when balancing a career and raising children? What are some things you have implemented?

Boundaries are supposed to be firm walls not open gates so it is important to stick to those you put in place. They should be designed to maximise your productivity, creativity and life in general.

Learning to say 'no' is the most obvious boundary and also the hardest one to learn. I have learnt to value my own time and the investment of quality time spent with the kids and family. Saying 'no' is not something that comes easily but practise really does make perfect. If I say 'yes' to everything I won't be able to give my best to each project. This is not only hard to take personally but is also detrimental to business. Clients really do understand this if you level with them. Most of the time it is not a flat out 'no', just a 'not now'.

I am also particularly selective with meetings. Most things these days can be arranged via phone or email and, although face-to-face is fantastic and how real business is done, it is difficult for me to get to meetings while the kids are at home. For me to attend a meeting requires a babysitter, travel time, parking fees and time away from my children, whereas it may be just a quick cup of coffee for the other person. When meetings are essential I usually plan them for just after our monthly breakfast in the city and do them all at once. I also invite clients and suppliers to networking meetings which is a great cost-effective way to entertain. Business associates really do understand my situation, which is certainly not unique, and have been fantastic throughout this period. When both kids are at school the situation will be easier, but for now this is the solution. You just do what you have to do.

Is there a significant quote or saying which you live your life by?

'Do it NOW!'

Being a full-time manager to my kids, home and business means I have to be ultra-efficient, but I can be a bit of a procrastinator at times so this saying has transformed my life. I say this to myself many, many times a day and it is a great motivator. Rather than having so many things going at once and doing a bit on everything I now sit down and completely finish one thing as often as I can. If I am tempted to put it aside and do something else then I tell myself to 'Do it now!' This applies to business, home and family as well.

I also embrace the saying, *'What goes around comes around'*. I am a firm believer in karma and believe that how you live your life today reflects what will happen to you tomorrow.

What do you think holds people back from achieving their goals?

First, we don't write them down and focus on them, and second we don't believe we can achieve them.

How many of us wander around and aimlessly network without really knowing what we are networking for? Sure, all of us know that we want to expand our range of contacts, unearth amazing people and expand our businesses or careers, but how many of us are absolutely clear on where our path is headed? I am incredibly guilty of having all these grand ideas and taking on too much at once. I have learnt the hard way that it is important to articulate, define and (in my case) contain your goals and work every day to achieve them.

These days I have a goals book where I write down all my goals in one section and business ideas in another. When I am absolutely clear that I want to move ahead with a business idea I will move it to the goals section. Then I revisit my goals book through an appointment with myself each month and see where I am and what I still have to do. Consistent effort is the key in my opinion. Even if the goal is a little far off at the moment at least if you have it clear in your mind then you can start attracting the right people and information and can refine the goal as you go.

The other obstacle is belief in ourselves. For some reason a lot of people consider themselves unworthy of greatness or unable to achieve great things. We are all built in the same way and can achieve whatever we want in life if we just believe we can. We need to surround ourselves with positive people who will encourage us rather than Doubting Thomases who will find every reason under the sun why your goal will fail. As far as aspirational goals about houses, cars, holidays, clothes and so forth go, pictures are always great – find something similar in a magazine and hang it somewhere you will see it every day, then visualise what life will be like when you are there. Focus and consistent effort coupled with belief will get you there. Meditation is also a great investment in yourself and allows your brain the time to slow down and focus properly.

Why do you believe that encouragement is so important?

We are too quick to put down someone who has upset or insulted us, too quick to make a negative comment about someone we don't like, too quick to get jealous and too quick to compete. There have been many studies done on the impact of positive parenting and encouraging children – why should adults be any different? Everyone responds better to a positive comment than a negative one. I am a firm believer in management from the bottom up, not the top down. Although some direction is important and required, a manager is there to support and guide staff and encourage the team to excel as a whole. A manager's role is to spot the passion and expertise in each individual and maximise this within the team and within the person.

Quite often people never fulfil their lifelong dream because they never thought they were 'good enough' to follow that path. But what if you had someone who said, 'Yes, you can do that and you will be great!' Someone who believed in you and encouraged you in everything you did. Someone who could listen to your wildest dreams and not laugh! Some people are lucky enough to have had these people in their lives, or at least to have the self-confidence to do it anyway, but there are many more who didn't or don't.

Who are the role models or mentors that have inspired you? What important lessons have you learnt from them?

My husband is a huge role model in my life. He taught me the power of patience and how to review an opportunity from all angles. I used to think I could do everything and would work myself to the bone. Now I review each opportunity for what it is and only pick those I can handle and can accommodate in my busy life. I think the secret to success is valuing your time, understanding your limitations and staying as stress-free as possible! Success is also about focusing on those projects that are truly worthwhile and valuable for your career or business. There are a lot of time-wasters out there!

Another role model is that crazy man who flies around in red and white planes! Sir Richard Branson lives his brand and manages to apply his brand philosophy to all areas of his business, regardless of how diverse they may be. By watching the progress of the Virgin Group and from reading his biography I have learnt

66 Another role model is that crazy man who flies around in red and white planes! 99

the value of a consistent brand message. Whatever business you run the underlying brand message and philosophy must be consistent and unshakeable. It must be like a sacred mantra that permeates all areas of the product, premises, staff and business in general.

What do you think we can do to build a better tomorrow?

Do whatever we can to protect our planet. Each small action adds up to a significant contribution if everyone does it. Do an audit of your home, business or workplace, and your life and see what changes you can make to conserve water, energy and waste. The smallest change can add up to significant savings over a year or more. Being environmentally aware isn't just a nice thing to do anymore – it's an absolute necessity. There are many ways to contribute but here are just a few to get you started:

- Change appliances to energy-saving ones or go back to the good old-fashioned way of doing things by hand. Hang clothes on the line instead of using the dryer (your clothes will last longer too).
- Wash clothes in cold water and use an environmentally friendly laundry liquid.
- Network on the go by picking up a colleague or two on the way to work rather than everyone driving their own car.
- Plant some native trees and drought hardy plants, and create an environment for native animals in your garden. If you don't have a garden, consider giving a gift of a tree to a friend who does.
- Don't drive to the shops – do yourself and the planet a favour and get some exercise! Try to leave the car at home one day per week.

The other thing we can do to create a better tomorrow is to be nice to each other. There is too much aggression in our society today. I so often see people being rude to the people they come across in their daily dealings and it really isn't necessary. Say thank you with a wave when driving if someone lets you go in front of them, say hello to the bus driver or shop assistant and ask them how they are. And perhaps most importantly – smile!

Throughout your career you have been committed to continual study. Why is that so important?

Everything changes so fast these days and we have so much going on in our lives that it is necessary to keep up with current trends and information. I also believe we need to stimulate our brains regularly – not just through study but also through many methods such as reading, mentoring relationships and solving problems. I love learning and enjoy both the process of study and the achievement at the end. Study also opens up new ways of doing things and new networks, which is always exciting. Although I am unable to tackle study head-on due to all of the other commitments in my life, I find that a small consistent effort is enough to keep the cogs working!

What advice would you give to someone living in a rural area that would like to start their own networking group?

Know your purpose – decide on the purpose for your network. Who is your target market? Why are you running it? Be clear on your reasons and articulate these in all material and advertising so that people know what to expect and why they should attend.

Start small – find a venue that will take numbers as they arrive, like a restaurant, then advertise the date, either through a press release to the local paper or another medium. Find a speaker who is well known in the community and is willing to share their knowledge. Call the local paper and invite a journalist to attend at no charge.

Listen to your network members – find out what each person attending that first event hopes to achieve by being a part of the network and listen intently to their answer. Capture the contact details of everyone attending and organise an even better follow-up event. Give guests an incentive to attend the next event with a friend and make them feel special as one of the inaugural network members.

> 66 Say thank you with a wave when driving if someone lets you go in front of them... 99

Find sponsors – to alleviate costs and help with promotions. Locate businesses that want to help the community and gain a presence for their brand through association with your event. Once you have a sponsor, stick to your agenda and be consistent in your product offering. Allowing your event or network to evolve in an organic way is fine, but don't jump all over the place with different themes and goals. This is confusing for a sponsor that has specific objectives.

Apart from all this – have FUN! A network is a place where people should feel comfortable and if *you* have fun and feel happy to be there, then so will your guests.

FREE BONUS GIFT

Kim McGuinness has kindly offered a FREE BONUS GIFT valued at $19.95 to all readers of this book...

Event-Specific Networking – In this special collection of articles, businesswoman and networking specialist Kim McGuinness shares a host of valuable tips to maximise your value and effectiveness when attending any function or event. By learning these powerful life skills, not only will you be able to create memorable interactions, but you'll learn to capitalise on those connections for mutual benefit.

Simply visit the private web page below and follow the directions to download direct to your Notebook or PC.

www.SecretsExposed.com.au/inspiring-women

DENISE HALL

66 What I have learnt is that being opportunistic and bold will get you so much further ahead, and will point you in directions where you can work out the rest! 99

DENISE HALL

Denise Hall was born in 1961, and grew up in the Olympic Village (post Games) in Melbourne. After completing her Higher School Certificate, she had no idea what she wanted to do and was not keen (at that time) to continue an 'institutionalised' education. Instead, she decided to get a job and earn some money.

After a few false starts, Denise's history of full-time, salary-paid employment was dominated by working for one of the top four banks in Australia followed by an international management consultancy. She officially 'retired' in 1997 when she eventually became disenchanted with working in the corporate jungle.

At the ripe old age of 36 Denise found herself unemployed, homeless, and pregnant. It was at this time that her entrepreneurial spirit was ignited. With some clever and rather fortunate business partnering, and some hard innovative work, Denise took over aCE talentNET on a national level and built a solid foundation for its successful growth. aCE talentNET is run entirely by entrepreneurial mothers, just like herself.

Denise believes that Frank Sinatra's song 'I did it my way' epitomises her journey to date and will no doubt continue to do so. She is not one to blindly follow others, but rather blazes her own individual trail, a fact that is evident in her story thus far.

How would you describe yourself as a person?

Mother, entrepreneur, counsellor, consultant, opportunist, decision-maker, mistake-maker, action-taker, lifelong learner, traveller, adventurer, innovator, designer (of life).

Tell us about your early career. What skills were you lacking and what did you do to make up for them?

I started out in the advertising game, but that didn't last long. I soon started 'playing' with a number of friends who had yet to land jobs post-school, and stayed on the dole for about six months to fund that fun and frivolity. When I got bored (and poor) I decided to do something about making real money and walked into a number of banks on the way home from the unemployment office. Within a week I was employed by the ANZ bank and planned to stay only until the next best thing came along. I left 13 years later, well and truly institutionalised (again!). Then the Total Quality Management (TQM) movement rolled into town, reaching its crescendo when I was in a position to be able to leap on board. I learnt a lot and thoroughly enjoyed it. At about the same time (and once I had found something of genuine interest) I went to university part-time and completed a Bachelor of Training and Development. This chain of events led to many opportunities and by the time I left to join Proudfoot Consulting, I was doing breakthrough innovative work implementing self-managed teams in the data processing environment.

I have found that whenever I am lacking in knowledge or skills I ask questions. If I ask the right questions of the right people, coupled with researching and reading pertinent information, I am bound to end up getting closer to where I want or need to go. For me, the key to moving forward starts with asking questions, finding out as much as I can, and then making a decision based on what I know at any given point in time.

> 66 It got messy and emotional and left me with a bad taste in my mouth. 99

Tell us about your work as an international management consultant. What exactly did you do?

My reason for leaving the safety of ANZ and starting a job in an area somewhat left of field like Proudfoot Consulting, was the chance to do a different type of work and to have the opportunity to travel the world at the same time. The job was primarily about working with clients to achieve a productive and well-driven business. It was about providing the implementation support necessary to achieve measurable and sustainable performance improvement, thus assisting clients to achieve their full potential (and in the process, to fulfil my own potential as well).

I learnt a great deal working for Proudfoot Consulting, it was a job that saw me work in underground coalmines, convenience stores in the Midwest of the US, a rubber glove manufacturing plant in Penang Malaysia, and many other adventurous and exciting places.

When did you know that it was time to move on?

On both counts, it has been when I came to the realisation that the role and organisation was not serving my fundamental needs for engagement and growth; the 'care factor' had gone missing!

About ten years into my tenure at ANZ the first of the now regular, major restructuring exercises rolled in. Having never been through such a thing before, no one knew what to expect or how to handle the process or the repercussions and fall out. It got messy and emotional and left me with a bad taste in my mouth. As a result, I vowed to myself that I would use the experience as a catalyst to find a new role in which I felt valued and 'loved' again. It took me approximately three years to do that.

At Proudfoot, after about four years of back-to-back projects, I negotiated six months leave without pay. I spent that time travelling in Greece, Turkey, Israel, Egypt and many more countries of Africa. Upon returning from that incredible adventure and getting back into work, I struggled badly. As a result, that job had to go too, actually any job for that matter – I wanted and needed to do my own thing!

You say that your life resembles the Frank Sinatra song, 'I did it my way'. What do you mean by that?

For the first 30 years of my life, I pretty much followed societal norms. After taking six months off work and returning from a cathartic adventure in Africa, I realised that things weren't right, and that I had to do it my way. This realisation probably had something to do with the 'ah ha' moment I experienced in Africa, and the conclusion that I didn't like where my life was heading and that I really wanted to do something about changing it upon my return. And change I did! Within a two-week period, I sold my apartment, resigned from a regular paying job, and had a pregnancy test confirmed. So all of a sudden, at the ripe old age of 36, I found myself unemployed, homeless and pregnant. Despite asking myself a lot of questions and going to hell and back a few times, I eventually got to a point where I knew I could do it, and I could do it my way.

To give a taste of what happened next, I opened myself up to opportunity and alternative ways of living and working – I was no longer going to follow the traditional path but rather find my own! I was able to secure my first solo consulting project (with a little morning sickness to add some colour) and arranged house-sitting gigs for most of my pregnancy while allowing my body to do its thing. All worked out swimmingly, and as for the future details, I continue to have fun working those out as I go!

Why did you start your own business and how did you choose what field to go into?

Wanting to do my own thing led me to my own business. At the outset, I was doing more of the same but on a much smaller, independent consulting scale. I was then approached by an ex-Proudfoot Consulting colleague about setting up a Melbourne office of the Sydney-based aCE talentNET (then aCE Resources). After much consideration, I came to the conclusion that it was a great opportunity, something I could do around my baby (being pregnant at the time) and a way of building an asset for the future…perfect!

As good fortune would have it, as my daughter has grown so has this business. I took over the entire aCE talentNET business in 2000 and it is now a lot bigger than me. It grows and thrives both nationally and internationally.

With your own business comes a need to be a smart money manager, how have you been able to do this?

A smart money manager indeed! It became evident that I needed to be one when I was not on a regular salary for the first time in my life (and doesn't *that* make you focus on money matters?!). I had to seriously review my financial responsibilities for myself *and* my child, so cash flow (current and future) did become a key consideration. I read many books and articles, attended seminars, talked to targeted and talented people, and progressively built a knowledge bank, which enables me to now feel reasonably comfortable when making financial decisions. Examples of key financial decisions that I have subsequently been responsible for are the development and growth of aCE talentNET; the purchase of three properties (one has since been sold); the trading of shares; the growth and sale of another small business; and the partial ownership of a racehorse (all at the same time as continuing to finance significant overseas trips for two). Not bad in ten years!

You believe that sometimes it's important to 'de-institutionalise' and unlearn in order to progress. What do you mean by that?

'De-institutionalisation' is something that I had to 'name' and learn when I was leaving corporate life (and also school for that matter). It's where you release yourself from the shackles of what you were taught to be true as being the only way to go about life or business. It's basically about purging groupthink and identifying, establishing and living your own thoughts. It's probably also a little bit about rediscovering the 'why' behind doing the things you used to get into trouble for. It's about standing on your own two feet and eventually being pleasantly surprised, encouraged and validated that you can. It's about realising that doing it your way is okay after all!

Do you believe that there is such a thing as a glass ceiling for women in business? If so what can one do about it?

Most of the women I know aim not necessarily to be an executive or to fill a high-profile job, but rather to live an authentic life. For some, living that authentic life involves high-profile jobs, and unfortunately there are not many organisations and companies that truly want to provide the support to facilitate that notion. Therefore, the women that are capable of being executives often leave and set up their own businesses (*à la* me). Daniel Pink, creator of *Free Agent Nation* says, 'The number of women becoming small business entrepreneurs is soaring – because for many, the best response to the glass ceiling is to exit through the side door'. I think the concept of the glass ceiling does exist because there has to be some reason why women are not invited to participate in an environment where they could add so much value. I know too many competent and capable women who

> 66 I read many books and articles, attended seminars, talked to targeted and talented people... 99

choose not to pursue the top end of town, as participation would mean not living their authentic life.

However, for those women who do want to break through the glass ceiling, I think they have to realise that gaining one of these positions, and making it work, is a team effort. It's about creating a well thought-out plan for making it happen. Surrounding yourself with a smart team is a more rewarding, more sustainable and real way to make it happen. Just because 'successful' others in the corporate world have done it their way for so long doesn't mean it's the right and only way. Work out a plan and continue to chip away at your goals. To quote Robert Kiyosaki, 'What you say is who you are, and what you think is who you are – push your reality and choose your own, otherwise someone else will'.

What steps did you take to get to where you are now?

Fundamentally, I broadened my horizons. That is, I:

- travelled
- took advantage of opportunities that presented themselves
- experienced many wonderful adventures from which to draw on
- read and read and read
- received formal education
- followed my nose and backed my decisions
- ran with the luck (but as they say, luck is where opportunity and hard work meet)
- took calculated risks!

Throughout your business success, you also raised a daughter. What issues, if any, did this present?

Having a daughter presented many issues to me as a businesswoman. The major shift was the focus from 'me' to 'us' and 'I' to 'we', and the resultant restructuring needed. In fact, having another human being solely reliant on me got me incredibly focused. And of course that worked hand-in-hand with treading new territory, exploring ways to earn money, creating a workable life mindful of having a dependent, and accentuating the need to back my own judgement even more. I was also (and still am) blessed that I had the loving support of family and friends through such tumultuous times. Sometimes they would roll their eyes at me and wonder what the hell I was doing. But I'm pleased to report that most have stayed with me for the ride.

What is the most important thing you have learnt about being a mother, role model and businesswoman?

I've learnt that all of these roles are important and that all of them require mastering the ability to 'go with the flow'. I tend to bundle these roles together because I don't believe there is a fundamental difference in what each is trying to achieve.

As Jack Welch says, 'Before you are a leader, success is all about growing yourself. When you become a leader, success is all about growing others'. Doesn't that apply to each of these roles? Isn't one of the key functions of being a mother to remove as many obstacles as possible to enable a child to grow into the human being they are capable of becoming? Is that not the same for role models and businesspeople alike? A mother's role is to love and nurture, is that not what is also required of role models and businesspeople? Granted, the 'love' element is in a different context and intensity, but isn't it worthy of similar consideration? Is it not one of the key functions of businesspeople to create relationships and processes that enable successes as frequently as possible? Is that not the same for mothers and role models as well?

For me, each of these roles is similar and therefore requires similar qualities for success.

> 66 ...being a role model worthy of respect is the best gift you can give your child. 99

You have some strong views about the current education system. What are they?

I believe that education is the key to living an authentic life on so many levels. Based on my personal education and now, my daughter's, I believe that we fall short in a number of areas. For example, we should be:

- addressing the curriculum in our schools (particularly delivery and content)
- including topics such as money and financial literacy; relationships and how to be good parents and partners; the mystery of love and sex (and that's just for starters).

Education is not about training people to be employable. It's about enabling them to be the person they are destined to be, to reach their full potential. It's not about finding oneself, it's about creating oneself. Heck, I still don't know what I want to be when I grow up!

There are only two things in life that one can truly invest – time and money. And with key adults in children's lives spending more of their time in other places and then throwing money at addressing the issue, who is really developing the children? And in what areas exactly? Where does that leave the children when they need to become adults?

In 2000/2001 I facilitated the national 'Australis Self Made Girl' programs around Victoria. The program introduced 14 to 18-year-old girls to the notion of economic empowerment and financial independence. It was a wonderful program and most fulfilling for all involved, but unfortunately the funding ran out and the program was canned. So who is teaching our girls, our friends, and even our mothers now?

Why is it so important? Because how will our children learn about such life skills if they are not fortunate enough to be surrounded by exceptional role models, which is sadly quite often the case? And please, I'm not saying it's the role model's fault. It's probably more to do with them not having access to fabulous role models either – but the cycle has to end somewhere. 'Children are our Common Wealth'.

What has been the greatest moment in your life so far and why?

I can boast many great moments but greatest by far is the birth of my daughter. Initially, it was about the awe I felt for the female human form and the capability held within. Now the awe that once defined this greatest moment has transformed into a sense of responsibility and a drive to be the best person I can be. I strongly believe that being a role model worthy of respect is the best gift you can give your child.

Denise and her daughter.

When I fell pregnant I made a decision early on that I would not read books (which is a complete contradiction to what I would normally do!) or learn anything about what should and should not be happening with my body and baby. In hindsight, this is a decision I'm really glad I made. Apart from the regular standard doctor appointments, I was travelling blind and trusting my instinct and body implicitly. As a result, I was able to truly enjoy the experience rather than worry about what may or may not be happening. Fortunately all worked out just fine and my beautiful daughter, Ireland, was born (she's now nine).

What do you think holds people back from achieving their goals?

When the characteristics of successful people have not been or are not being cultivated, goal creation and achievement will be held back. Therefore, you run the risk of not doing what you want to do because you are too fearful, and/or because you are not confident enough to believe you can. But it doesn't have to stay that way. If identifying and achieving goals is a true driver, then educating yourself by finding out ways, means and tools to do just that will assist in getting you where you want to go. If you don't have age on your side (and let's be honest, sometimes that doesn't help!), then find talented, sharing people who do.

What do you think has been the secret to your accomplishments thus far?

Would you believe it – age! Or perhaps a better word is 'cultivation'. By that I mean becoming a more educated and more rounded human being. It's about making the most of your time.

Given that I went through the same education system as most others (and presumably a fairly similar parental system too), I believe my education was completed without really having the tools I needed to have a major go at living. I did not truly understand how, or even if, I could stand on my own two feet. I've had to work that out for myself. Fortunately, I have been around long enough now to have had amazing highs, coupled with flat spots, and done many things to ground myself so I can continue to launch. Let's face it, it's not always in the best interest of institutions, such as schools and large corporations, to teach and train what it truly means to be entrepreneurial and to follow dreams.

What I have learnt is that being opportunistic and bold will get you so much further ahead, and will point you in directions where you can work out the rest! I have also been blessed by being surrounded by people who support and love in ways that continue to inspire me.

Did you ever reach a point where it became difficult and you considered giving up? What kept you fighting?

'Giving up' as such just doesn't register with me. However, if I do find myself in a position where life is not turning out as planned, then I simply ask myself, 'How can I change this? This is not working for me; what do I need to creatively do to either make it work or make it go away?'

There was a period in my life when I tried to resign myself to a life less authentic by maintaining a relationship that was losing its reason for being. The more I tried to do that though, the more and more I struggled, which ultimately led to the demise of that particular liaison anyway. Eventually I got to the question, 'Is this as good as it gets?' The answer was a deafening 'NO' and I was able to manage the 'feeling' part, I was then able to 'think' through and define steps, which when committed to and followed, showed me the way onwards and upwards.

What is the biggest mistake you have made and how did 'going with the flow' help you overcome it?

I define a mistake as a 'mis-take'. Fortunately, my life has been a never-ending series of mis-takes, as they are what I have used to chart my life's course.

> 66 I now have an innate belief that all works itself out as it needs to. 99

tully ©

The situation I placed myself in at 36 could have ended up being my biggest mis-take, however, I have learnt (and continue to learn) that going with the flow is the real and only way to live. I now have an innate belief that all works itself out as it needs to. It's not the mis-take that matters, it's the recovery. One of the main responsibilities of my life is to set sail, strive to 'do it my way' and, in essence, enjoy the ride!

In your opinion what are the characteristics that make a successful person?

To borrow heavily from Dr Martyn Newman (and his research) of *Emotional Capitalists – The New Leaders* fame, much of it is about emotional intelligence and more specifically about:

- *Independence* – self-belief and self-reliance.
- *Assertiveness* – giving clear messages and having self-control.
- *Optimism* – looking for the benefits and possibilities and seeing valuable lessons.
- *Self-actualisation* – having a passion for what you do and creating the life you want.
- *Self-regard* – self-liking and self-competence.
- *Interpersonal relationships* – treating others as equals, creating win-win situations for all, and providing autonomy.
- *Empathy* – understanding what others want to achieve and the emotional dimensions involved.

If you had your time over again is there anything you would do differently?

I could contemplate what might have been by going through some of the lessons I've learnt, but would I have had the maturity to learn from them? Who can say? What I know for sure is that I am the person I am today because of the life I have lived thus far…and you know what? That's okay!

Is there a significant quote or saying which you live your life by?

Based on the vast amount of material I have absorbed over the years, I have a million of them, from a variety of inspiring people. A selection of my favourites include:

- *'Someone else's opinion of you is none of your business!'*
- *'Feel the fear and do it anyway.'*
- *'The pain is in the indecision.'*
- *'Break it down into do-able tick-box chunks.'*
- *'If someone shows you who they are, believe them.'*
- *'Don't fall in love with potential.'*
- *'Imagination is one thing; action is another.'*
- *'You can't 'think' when you 'feel'.'*

- *'We can never outperform the image we have of ourselves.'*
- *'Hope is not a strategy.'*
- *'It is our choices that show what we truly are, far more than our abilities.'*

What are some of your goals for the next five years?

I always have goals and plans listed in some form or another (I am a journal writer from way back). I usually critically review those around New Year, and tinker with them along the way if need be. Key headings I review (thanks to David Schirmer – now of *The Secret* fame) are:

- family life
- social life
- business life
- income
- education
- health
- spiritual life

It does sound rather structured, doesn't it? Still, I find it a most worthwhile and rewarding exercise to do. It always surprises me how far my thinking can shift within a 12-month period.

What are your five favourite books?

Being the insatiable reader that I am, and having the library of books that I do, choosing only five is very difficult.

- *The Power of One* – Bryce Courtney
- *Emotional Capitalists* – Dr Martyn Newman
- *If you want to be Rich and Happy, Don't go to School* – Robert Kiyosaki
- *Re-imagine!* and *The Essentials* – Tom Peters
- *Free Agent Nation* – Daniel Pink

From your many years of experience, what advice would you give to others about change?

- Feel the fear and do it anyway!
- Embrace it!
- Live and breathe it!
- Enjoy it and have fun with it!
- Bring it on!

Where do you see yourself in 20 years' time?

Swanning around the world as I please, playing grandmother, receiving bucketloads of passive income, and being healthy, wealthy and wise!

What do you love most about being where you are today?

That I was and I am capable of participating in life, in its many and varying forms. The comfort of knowing that my history is providing the catalyst for creating my present and my future is most reassuring.

At the end of your life how do you want to be remembered?

I would like to think that the people I have come into contact with have been genuinely better off for the experience. I also want to be remembered for epitomising 'love' in action. A tough want to aspire to, I agree, but one I believe to be well worth the effort.

FREE BONUS GIFT

Denise Hall has kindly offered a FREE BONUS GIFT valued at $19.95 to all readers of this book...

The Entrepreneurial Mother's Guide To Working Out What You Want – Denise Hall is the director of aCE talentNET which focuses on performance improvement. As her company is run almost entirely by entrepreneurial women, she has collected a host of tried and tested strategies designed to help working women maximise their productivity, while at the same time creating a better quality of life. Formatted as a handy workbook, this bonus will not only benefit you but those around you as well.

Simply visit the private web page below and follow the directions to download direct to your Notebook or PC.

www.SecretsExposed.com.au/inspiring-women

Sally Anderson

SALLY ANDERSON

66 The fact that I survived with no support to cope with what happened is nothing short of a miracle. I now have the honour and joy of spending the rest of my life giving back what I have learnt. Therein lies the gift! 99

SALLY ANDERSON

Sally Anderson was born in 1965 in Tokoroa, New Zealand. She spent four of her early years in Vancouver, Canada, (where she learnt to ski) before returning to New Zealand and spending her childhood growing up in Ohope, in the Bay of Plenty. Her mother was a teacher for the intellectually disabled and her father was a guidance counsellor within the secondary school system. A visionary ahead of his time, his contribution to youth reform, and latterly aquaculture in New Zealand, left a formidable legacy.

At the age of 15, Sally was abducted and gang raped by the Mongrel Mob (a New Zealand gang) in one of the worst reported attacks of its kind in New Zealand in the early eighties. In 2004, her story of survival, courage and transformation was profiled on New Zealand *60 Minutes*. Her story is an extraordinary testament to human survival and commitment to the highest level of human performance against all odds.

Her determination to regain her life following this trauma led to Sally immersing herself in a range of courses for over 20 years, and as a result she has been trained in a broad cross section of personal development curricula.

Today, Sally is a prominent futurist, visionary and behavioural specialist. She has established a unique coaching organisation in Auckland, New Zealand, that specialises in executive coaching, legacy leadership and transformational seminars focused on the advancement of human performance.

At 15 years of age you went through a horrific experience. Can you explain what happened to you?

When I was 15 I thought I had gained my independence – I got a job. It was my first job during the school holidays at a national park ski lodge. I thought I was 'the bee's knees', on my own, independent for the first time and earning my own money at last! After I got my first pay packet, a girlfriend and I planned a day outing in Taumarunui, and in celebration of our newfound independence we hitchhiked all the way from the ski lodge. We felt excited and quite grown-up (although I was still pretty young) and found ourselves chatting away to the locals at a public bar. We were enjoying ourselves and lost track of time. Well, I lost track of time – my girlfriend was no longer with me. I searched the pub, but she was nowhere to be found. Then I realised that my bag was mysteriously missing as well. Alarmed, I ventured outside and down the alleyway adjacent to the pub. No one was there. What I didn't realise was that I had been cased out by the Mongrel Mob as their fresh piece of meat. Suddenly a car pulled up outside the public bar, I was thrown inside and my nightmare began.

As the car sped off toward the outskirts of town, the streetlights dimly illuminated the faces of eight fierce-looking men. Terror struck me as I glimpsed the prominent tattoos covering their bodies, the chains slung over their shoulders and chests, and the scruffy jeans and leather jackets – Mongrel Mob members! But what scared me even more were the leering looks on their faces. Where were they taking me? Before I knew it we had arrived at a dilapidated old house on the outskirts of town, I was wrenched from the car and one of the men dragged me through the silent, empty house into one of the bedrooms. He threw me on the unmade bed and started to grope me as I vainly tried to fend him off. Despite his intoxicated state, he was still very large and strong and all I could do was reel away from his fetid breath. Overwhelmed with terror, I couldn't fight. I couldn't even scream.

❝ I was pulled off the workbench and thrown into a utility truck with five men. ❞

It seemed like a very long time. The end was indicated only when my attacker slumped on top of me in a drunken stupor. Now was my chance to escape. I saw the window just above the bed and desperately tried to ease myself from under the man's dead weight. Just as I did, any plan of escape was quenched as four more gang members came storming in. They dragged me out of the house and into a garage filled with men drinking, smoking and blaspheming. I still remember the heavy smoke in the air, and the smell of their sweat and excitement. As they threw me facedown on a wooden workman's bench, they proceeded to rip the clothes off my body. I was paralysed. My nightmare continued for more than ten hours, and as I closed my eyes, I could still feel the depravity of their animalistic actions. I could still hear the men egging each other on and cajoling others to get involved. I just wanted to die. I could no longer cope with the reality of the situation – I had lost my virginity in the most brutal manner and the agony of the battering seemed to never end. I was viciously and roughly attacked vaginally, anally and orally – taking me beyond the limits of my endurance, both physically and mentally. And still they continued to rape me.

As I began to question God's existence, I was pulled off the workbench and thrown into a utility truck with five men. Where was this God? What had I done to deserve this? Driven to another location, I was continually abused by the men who took turns, ferociously taking pleasure in the rape of a defenceless 15-year-old girl. I felt totally lifeless. I was still naked, covered in bruises and so angry – with me! Why didn't I fight back? Why didn't I scream? You could have screamed! What's wrong with you? It was early morning when we reached another house. Left alone for a few minutes in the back of the ute, I thought about escaping, but I was in shock. I was too terrorised to move in case they caught me and inflicted even more cruelty on me. Only minutes passed before three of my captors returned and hauled me into the house. They dumped me in one of the bedrooms and the abuse continued.

I had endured so much, and had been stripped of all dignity. Was I even human now? I was going crazy, and yet throughout my whole ordeal I had remained conscious. I was aware of everything that happened to me.

How did you find the energy and courage to escape your attackers?

I didn't. And I'm not sure I would have. The horrific abuse ended when the boss of the mob arrived back at the house. I was unable to comprehend the irony of the situation as he and his partner found me some old jeans and a grubby sweater, and then drove me back to Taumarunui. Neither of them spoke to me during the drive, apart from asking me where I was staying. They then dropped me on the side of the road outside the lodging house and demanded money. At their insistence, I picked myself up and walked through the back entrance of the lodge, into the kitchen and woodenly said to the young kitchen-hand that I needed $20. My dishevelled appearance shocked him into silence. The fact that I was desperate and humiliated was clearly obvious and I could not even try to explain what had happened. He asked no questions, but gave me the money. I hobbled back to the waiting car and they took the money and sped off.

By this time I had been missing for 36 hours. I was left standing in the middle of a national park on a cold winter's night, battered and torn (inside and out). I fell to my knees, convinced I was losing my mind.

Is it true that the morning after being attacked, you went to work?

On the night of returning to the lodge, I sat in a bath and vigorously scrubbed myself raw. I felt so alone, confused, lost, insane, vulnerable and scared. I was working on mentally erasing everything that had transpired over those 36 hours. To preserve my sanity I had to act as if it hadn't happened. I couldn't comprehend the reality of what had happened to me, so in order to survive I assumed a façade from that moment on. The person I had been died at the age of 15. The next morning I got up and went to work as if nothing had happened. I had assumed my new façade but I had not taken into account my appearance. When I arrived at work my horrified colleagues took one look at me and called the police. At that point my frail defences collapsed and I broke down and told them as much as I could.

How did people respond to you, as you relived the trauma of your rape?

The police were very efficient but I was in a state of shock and felt so alone, alienated and humiliated that I was unable to respond with any emotion. I then had to undergo a thorough medical examination (further humiliation and pain) and although the doctor was kind, the whole process felt very clinical. I could not make eye contact with anyone as the police questioned me over and over. While I knew they were only doing their job, I was desperately trying to forget. I did not want to be reminded of what had happened.

When my parents arrived at Taumarunui to take me home, I felt very distant and withdrawn. I felt I had brought shame on them. After all, I knew I shouldn't have been in the pub in the first place. So perhaps it was my fault? Had I deserved it? Throughout the long drive home I had no idea what my parents were feeling or thinking and there was silence in the car as we were all lost in our own thoughts. I was ashamed and wondered whether they would still love me. I couldn't let anyone touch me and I was a complete mess inside. The vicious self-talk was constant and I didn't know how to turn it off.

How did you cope with the aftermath of your attack?

I didn't care much for rape counselling – what would they know? – I hadn't just been raped by one person. I hated thinking like that, but I couldn't help myself. When I returned to school some weeks later, I opened up to a close friend whom I trusted. I realised the dichotomy of wanting to forget but also wanting to tell someone what I had experienced. In order to mentally handle the aftermath I literally began to wonder whether it actually happened. In fact, as I had not suffered any physical disfigurement, my mind decided that because externally what had happened was not evident to the naked eye, then it couldn't have occurred. I had often felt 'different', and given my already well-entrenched dislike of my appearance (my carrot-red hair and white freckled skin), this experience finally closed down any possibility of self-esteem, self-love or feelings of self-worth. Who would want a woman like me? I was so disgusted with myself, that had my body been infested with maggots it could not even come close to the bitter hatred I felt for myself for many years. I often wondered, how does a human being live on this planet after such an ordeal and relate to the average person? Having gone beyond the threshold of pain, I felt I could not relate to others who would have no understanding of how one could feel after such a horrific experience.

I wanted to die, and this became a familiar thought over the next 20 years when I contemplated suicide many times. I didn't want to be here and I didn't know how to relate to anyone anymore. The coping mechanism I adopted was to wipe the tape and act as if it didn't happen – but it did!

Did the police ever find your attackers?

The police found three of the men who had abducted me and driven me to the mob's hangout in Te Kuiti, and one year later I appeared in court. The thought of appearing in front of them in court was abhorrent to me and I wanted nothing to do with the trial. I was not interested in revenge, and felt the whole process was a waste of time. I had no time to think about the offenders, I was too busy trying to deal with my own

> 66 The person I had been died at the age of 15. 99

sanity! I had effectively internalised all of my anger and was methodically taking it out on myself.

My father accompanied me to court, but I did not want my mother to attend and hear the gruesome details of what had happened. It was hard enough that my father was present as they related the events that had taken place. Knowing that I smoked, my father asked me if I wanted a cigarette before the trial. I will never forget that. He knew what it was going to take to get through the court case.

Although two of the mob members were sentenced to eight years in jail, I felt that I had been the one on trial! I had to substantiate everything, right down to what I was wearing. It was even suggested that I had been 'sexually attired'. I could not imagine that wearing a *Starsky and Hutch*-style knee-length woollen jumper, corduroy trousers, and Ugg boots could be construed as being sexually dressed. It all felt so wrong! The questions were fired at me rapidly like an interrogation with little or no empathy shown towards me.

After spending so many years trying to forget the events of your attack, you now share your experience with other people. Why do you choose to do this?

I know of three other gang rapes in New Zealand, which I understand were of the same level of viciousness. Two of the victims committed suicide and the other person was committed to a mental institution. Why was I spared? Now I have found my voice and I choose to spend the rest of my life encouraging other people to find theirs, regardless of what their past has dealt them.

I have been asked over the years, when sharing this story, why I would disclose something so horrific. As someone who has endured and survived, I understand that society prefers not to take responsibility for the fact that acts of this nature do occur. However, I know how important it is that people find the courage to speak of their experiences, and that they are heard. I know all too well that to internalise pain and anguish is not healthy – for anyone.

Apparently at the point of trauma your body disassociates from your inner consciousness, and in some instances never reintegrates back into being whole and complete. I feel privileged that I have experienced the full cycle of reintegration and that I am here today to be able to share my experiences. However, this was not always the case. I spent many years travelling the world, disconnected from the inner me, while at the same time searching for answers outside of me. For answers I looked to the next book, personal development course, business mentor, expert or consultant, and was always disillusioned because none ever met my expectations. I then tried the self-destructive methods of excessive drinking, smoking, drugs, destructive relationships, and promiscuity. I believed that by avoiding or operating over the top of my pain and fear I could somehow find a solution. I was wrong! I did not know then that it would be my journey within that would alter my life. To say we are the source of our own enlightenment is an understatement. I feel the wealthiest I have ever felt with what I now know. I realise that this is 'it', that there is nowhere to get to. All that exists is now, the present moment.

I feel privileged to be able to declare that I have found my voice, and I now wish to spend the rest of my life partnering others in the discovery of their own inner counsel. I have found that living an almost totally controlled life does not produce the most desirable results. I had thought that power came with being in control. I now realise that vulnerability is the true source of power. Synchronicity, serendipity, the magic of the moment can only occur when you relinquish control and surrender. I would not wish what I experienced on my worst enemy, but I am alive for a reason.

I feel privileged to have survived. The fact that I survived with no support to cope with what happened is nothing short of a miracle. I now have the honour and joy of spending the rest of my life giving back what I have learnt. Therein lies the gift!

> **66** I'm very present to the cost of more than 20 years of self-abuse. **99**

I have now come to understand that being gang-raped by more than 100 mob members, plus the additional 20 years of self-abuse, were actually my apprenticeship to do what I do today. I now understand the addicted person, I can walk in the shoes of those with no self-love, I now relate to the person who no longer wishes to be here. Years of vicious inner-critic dialogue, to the point where it nearly drove me to madness, have provided me with the opportunity to train people in how to master their inner critic!

Can you explain what the 'inner critic' is?

To be human is to have an inner critic. Much has been written on the subject but after a great deal of research, I have not found anything that speaks of what I am about to write here. I often use the term 'mastery'. But when I use it I am not talking about managing or coordinating around that inner voice, I am talking about silencing it so that you never hear it again. What could be possible in your life if you no longer experienced this destructive internal voice? Different people experience their inner critic to varying degrees. Some are not aware that certain addictive behaviours are actually a form of escapism from this destructive voice. Addictions like smoking, eating, drinking, busyness, drugs, promiscuity, inability to relax, in fact anything that removes them from being present to their emotions, serve the purpose well. The human psyche will create ways of silencing that voice at all costs. So when someone states that they do not have an inner critic, I know that in their world that is the case, because they will have adopted alternative structures to mask it. I had one of the most powerful inner critics known to man, and learning to overcome it was my apprenticeship for partnering others in learning how to master theirs. I didn't know it was possible to silence that inner voice until I learnt that 'anything you are unable to be with will have you'.

The first step in mastering the inner critic is to be able to 'be with' the voice, with no resistance. In Western society, when things come at us in life we have a tendency to defend, which in turn creates conflict. In Eastern philosophies we learn that when things come at you to deflect and go with the path of least resistance, thereby deflecting conflict.

When did the inner critic become manageable for you?

When I learnt that I was a victim at age 30. Not the easiest thing to come to terms with but I have since learnt that until you own where you are operating, you are unable to experience transformation.

You eventually met with a leading member of the Mongrel Mob on the television program 60 Minutes. What was that experience like?

For me it was completion. I believe that the only person who loses in the inability to forgive is the person that cannot forgive. I had already given 20 years of my life to this. Most people believe forgiveness is about forgiving the other party. I believe ten per cent of forgiveness belongs to the other party, and the other 90 per cent belongs to yourself. People often ask how I sustain what I advocate. That's easy. I'm very present to the cost of more than 20 years of self-abuse.

Were there any times that you wanted to give up? What got you through?

For over 18 years I experienced suicidal feelings and there were many times when I felt that I did not want to live anymore. The only thing that stopped me committing suicide was my brother, Mark. He died at the age of 23. I saw the devastating effect his death had on my parents and our family. As a parent you believe you will outlive your children. I could not put them through another death. So my brother pulled me through every time.

What is one of the biggest mistakes you've ever made in your life and what did you learn from it?

For many years I journeyed with no boundaries in my life and found many forms of escapism in addictive behaviours. I now have compassion for those lost years – the learning curve was steep. It took a lot of effort to learn about the power of boundaries and the power of healing.

One of your sayings is 'Does it hurt enough yet?' Can you explain this and give a few examples?

It has always fascinated me that it takes some kind of wake-up call (such as bankruptcy, a heart attack, the death of a loved one, a cancer scare) for some people to get a sense of urgency about their life. What is it about the human psyche that requires pain to be the motivator for us to reassociate with our emotions? When I speak about a sense of urgency, I do not mean trying to get somewhere other than where you are. I am speaking about passion. I asked someone recently what they were passionate about and their response was, 'Oh, I think passion is totally overrated'. For me, passion is the core of experiencing a phenomenal life. The velocity with which you apply yourself to life will be the velocity at which life comes at you. In my observation people tolerate a great deal. Every day we operate over the top of things that persistently aggravate us. We seem to be numb to the impact that such tolerances have in our lives. Imagine a life where you are able to sustain a state of heightened exhilaration!

Why is it that not everyone is interested in unrecognisable transformation? If you knew the formula to evolve to the highest potential of your existence in this lifetime, why would you not jump at the chance to experience it? I believe we do not even realise how unaware we are of the way we live life below the radar. We tend to live our lives disempowered by perceived circumstances. Enlightenment is a function of waking up to the unlimited potential available to all of us – if only we ask:

- Who am I really?
- What do I really stand for in this lifetime?
- When will I start fulfilling this journey?
- What do I want to be known for?
- What's stopping me from evolving to my highest potential?

People experience unnecessary pain in their relationships, in their careers, in their families, in their friendships, in their own internal dialogue – you name it. How painful does it need to be before transformation can take place? We intuitively get the tap on the shoulder, but we tend to ignore the first promptings of our intuition, so then we get the four-by-two to the back of the head. It hurts, but hey, we are used to it so we continue to ignore the warning signs until eventually we receive the 'Mack truck experience' – the wake-up call. What will it take to listen to our internal signals when we receive that tap on the shoulder? I believe we must surrender to living a life above the radar. In living life disassociated from our emotions, we do not have to show up on this planet in our full magnificence. What would your life look like if you did not tolerate anything? There would be nothing to complain about, and it would end the cycle of being serious, significant and dramatic as a way of being. When the noise of disassociation dissipates, you will start hearing a whole new level of possibility. Are you willing to listen?

What is default behaviour?

I believe moment by moment people are either in their default-based identity or their power-based identity. The default-based identity is what sends someone into a disempowered state. Beliefs and values are formed in childhood, and then form the basis for your behaviour, which in turn creates the structures that you place in your life. These structures influence the culture by which you choose to live your life and the consequent results that you experience.

> 66 ... eventually we receive the 'Mack truck experience' – the wake-up call. 99

It is called the 'default', for this is the state you automatically experience when you feel disempowered. There are four key areas that send a person into a disempowered state:

1. Fear.
2. Issues, problems and challenges.
3. Inner critic (destructive inner dialogue).
4. Confusion.

What would your life look like if you were no longer stopped by fear? If you no longer lived into issues, problems and challenges? If you were able to silence your destructive inner dialogue so that you no longer experienced it? And what would your life look like if you sourced all your answers from within? Now that's living an empowered life!

How can people live a life of heightened exhilaration?

Heightened exhilaration will be experienced when:

- You get present to what you are truly passionate about and then live that passion!
- Your purpose in life calls you forth far greater than you know yourself.
- You give yourself permission to reclaim your power in areas of your life that aren't working.
- You exemplify energetically how you wish to be perceived in the world.
- You no longer allow circumstances to alter your state.
- You experience the power of emanating a presence.
- You no longer allow the past to rule your future.
- You address the things that you tolerate.
- You allow yourself to feel and be vulnerable, for this is truly where the power lies.
- You value who you are in the world and put the oxygen mask on yourself first!

Why is it so important to remain in the present and how do people do that?

We are brought up in a society that trains us to strive for a future. People seek validation in their self-worth through external goals. However, what frequently happens is that the goal never quite matches our expectations. Our barometer for our level of happiness is therefore always reliant on external circumstances that are constantly shifting. I am not discounting the importance of achieving goals, but I *am* contesting living in a world where there is always somewhere else to get to. To sustain any level of happiness or satisfaction in this life does not, contrary to popular opinion, lie in the achievement of goals. I propose that it's important to charter your 'boat' (you and your goals) in the direction you wish to head, but not be attached to the outcome. This is where most people experience dissatisfaction, because the outcomes do not meet their expectations.

The daily thoughts of most people are either past-based or future-based. In other words, we are hardly ever present. This is a human phenomenon. Every day I listen to people saying they are 'not there yet', or they are 'getting there'. But where are they trying to get to? The fact is, there is nowhere to get to. That 'one day' in the future doesn't exist. This is 'it', here and now. The past is but a thought and the future is an illusion, a projection from the moment that is now.

What does Sally Anderson Limited (SAL) do to help people?

I feel one of the biggest perceived challenges facing humanity, not just women, is the ability to sustain an empowered life. If you knew you could sustain being in your power 24/7, would you not want access to knowing how? At SAL we teach people how to do precisely that. For example, your conscious mind recognises when fear is present. It then evaluates when you last felt it and based on that memory you experience a sensation. You then react, based on the past-based experience. At SAL we train you to rewire the first two stages of conscious cognition. The entire re-evaluation

> 66 Most people do not realise how disassociated they are from their emotions. 99

process liberates people to take their power back so they no longer live life consequent to circumstances.

We believe sustainability is the missing piece in most coaching/personal development programs in the marketplace. You go to a course, get that shot of euphoria, then you go back to your life – back to same old, same old. At SAL we give you the tools to use to sustain change and we advocate both personally and professionally that if you wish to invest money into change, let's make sure it is sustainable!

Tell us about the work you do now and how your approach may differ from that of a traditional coach?

Standard coaching is predominantly focused externally on the areas of your life you wish to transform, for example your business, your relationships and so on. This is a generalisation but we at SAL perceive the process as being quite head-based (that is, quite analytical, or what we term 'prescriptive'). Coaches will tell you that there is a lot to do in your life and business to get it to where you want it to be. We believe there is far more to coaching than this project management-type approach. This approach is focused on external action. Most people already have a very long list of things to do in their lives so the last thing we wish to do is add to that list. Is this project management model effective? Yes. Will you achieve your goals using this model? Yes. Is it sustainable? Not in our opinion!

At SAL we are primarily focused on who people are 'being', not what they 'do'. Our focus is 100 per cent on the person and we are only interested in shifting the individual experientially (by that I mean back to a feeling space). We believe that the key to sustaining change is to integrate the learning in an experiential fashion. Most people do not realise how disassociated they are from their emotions.

Our approach is heart-based and internally-focused. We teach sustainability tools so that the individual is able to sustain the change of their own accord without having to rely on any external mechanism. We coach holistically, so that we focus on every area of a person's life. Most coaches will focus on the domain that the person perceives is not working. At SAL we identify what you want to alter, but instead of focusing on the symptom, we address the cause. By resolving the cause the domain sorts itself out through osmosis. For example, to transform the business domain we focus on who you are 'being' in the business. Any prescriptive action taken is done from a state of 'being' which is a completely different approach to taking prescriptive action from a state of 'doing'.

You also do a lot of speaking engagements. What are some of your main messages?

- Always remember it is a profound privilege to be in the presence of another human being.
- It's not about the happening, it's how you *deal* with the happening that counts.
- If you are going to invest money into change make sure it is sustainable.
- Shift who you are being and by osmosis your world will shift.

What advice would you give to other women that have gone through something traumatic in their lives?

1. Allow people to support you.
2. Seek healing of an experiential nature.
3. Allow the grieving process to take place.
4. Seek counsel to talk through what you are feeling – do not shut down on your emotions. Feel whatever it is that needs to be expressed.
5. Nurture yourself.
6. Forgive yourself.
7. Know that you are never given anything in this lifetime that you cannot handle.

8. Know that wounds do heal and that you are a spiritual being having a human experience.

9. Focus on that which empowers you – you are not your past, you are not your thoughts.

10. Choose whether you will be a victim or gain wisdom from your experience – honour the perfection in all things.

Is there a significant quote or saying which you live your life by?

I believe that everything is always in perfection, so the mantra that I apply in my life is *'If this is perfect right now, who do I need to be in this moment?'* It enables me to stay centred and connected at all times.

 # FREE BONUS GIFT

Sally Anderson has kindly offered a FREE BONUS GIFT valued at $100 to all readers of this book...

Four Key Guiding Principals Of Living An Empowered Life – Sally Anderson truly has been to hell and back, however she managed to turn an extremely negative experience into a positive one, becoming a Legacy Coach and guiding people through life and all its challenges. This downloadable audio presentation speaks of the four guiding principles of living an empowered life. If you knew how to live a life where you always felt empowered, what could you accomplish?

Simply visit the private web page below and follow the directions to download direct to your Notebook or PC.

www.SecretsExposed.com.au/inspiring-women

SIMONE PRESTON

66 The mind is such a powerful instrument and keeping positive about myself is something that I work on every day...If I feel down, I distract myself with a reward – usually shopping for shoes or chocolate. 99

SIMONE PRESTON

Simone Preston was born in Kogarah, Sydney, in 1969 and grew up in Greenacre with her mum Kerrie, stepfather Greg, and brothers Dean and Curt.

She began working behind the bars of many well-known Sydney pubs, and later worked as a secretary, a salesperson and a sales and marketing manager. In 2005, Simone made the decision to start her own business. After attending many women's networks in major cities, she realised that there was a lack of business support for women in regional areas. So following some extensive market research she started Business Women Connect (BWC) – a networking group that provides forums to empower women with the skills to develop themselves professionally and personally and to realise their entrepreneurial capabilities.

Launching the company with a small database, a laptop, and a desk at home, Simone used her extensive network on the NSW Central Coast to start BWC. The first luncheon attracted over 150 attendees and received the necessary feedback to encourage Simone to further develop her business. One-and-a-half years later, BWC has expanded into five major regional areas and is forecasting a multimillion-dollar turnover in 2007.

As founder and managing director of BWC, Simone has combined her dual desires of running a successful business and empowering like-minded women to fully develop their potential. Her passion and drive have enabled her to build a company that has provided thousands of women in regional areas with the opportunity to be inspired by successful women from all over Australia. These breakfasts, luncheons, conferences, workshops and seminars have provided an avenue for women to develop the business skills necessary for success in today's competitive environment.

What were some of your early influences in life?

My Dad. I didn't realise the extent of his success as a young girl, my father actually played first grade footy for St George. He was regarded as a leading goal kicker, winger and fullback in his time but he was soon forgotten at the end of his stellar career. Nevertheless, he didn't give up and transferred his sporting ability to new business ventures. I wanted to be just like him – not to play football (although I think I inherited his football legs) – but to do whatever it took when times got hard and to not give up. I ended up working in my Dad's business and five things that he taught me were:

- be the best that you can be
- don't put too many expectations on yourself that you aren't going to achieve
- if something negative happens, look at how you can turn it into a positive
- learn from those around you
- don't ever give up!

What has been one of the biggest challenges you have faced in your life and how did you overcome it?

Having a baby at the age of 23 was my biggest challenge, especially when all of my friends were out partying. For the first six months after my son, Cooper, was born everything was fine. After that, the man that I thought I was going to spend the rest of my life with left, and my parents didn't take me back into the family home (not feeling sorry for me was the best thing my family did for me). My life was put into a complete spin! But I picked myself up and moved in with a friend in a similar circumstance. I put Cooper into childcare and got a job as a full-time receptionist – 18 hour days quickly became tiring. What kept me motivated was knowing that I had a supportive network of friends and family. I was never afraid to ask for help. I tried keeping up with friends by going to nightclubs and meeting new people, but I would usually have a few too many champagnes and still have to get up to a baby in the morning.

> **❝ She wasn't famous, but her status quickly escalated as she told her life's story. ❞**

To make things a little more complicated, by the age of two Cooper had already been kicked out of five different childcare centres. Apparently he was too active, wouldn't sit still, was full of beans... Was it his hearing? His eyesight? Did he have autism? As it happened, he had tendencies toward all three. After visiting a specialist on Attention Deficit Disorder (ADD), the doctor took one look at Cooper and immediately diagnosed him with Attention Deficit Hyperactivity Disorder (ADHD). He needed to be medicated. Putting your son on such powerful drugs at two-and-a-half is very scary – but it worked. Cooper is now 13 and has turned into a lovely young boy.

Is there a significant quote or saying which you live your life by?

When I was 25 years old, I attended a conference with a theme relating to the Olympic spirit – 'Dare to Dream'. The Athens Olympic Games were around the corner and the conference had invited Olympic champion Lisa Curry-Kenny to speak, along with other motivational guests. One woman who spoke, Janine Shepherd, used to train as a cross-country skier. I have to admit that when this lady stood up to speak, she looked quite normal and I began to wonder how her story was going to compare to someone like Lisa Curry-Kenny. She wasn't famous, but her status quickly escalated as she told her life's story.

One afternoon, while bike riding through the Blue Mountains in preparation for the Winter Olympics, Janine Shepherd's life was altered irrevocably when she was hit by a truck! Doctors warned her parents that she was not expected to survive – in fact, the bleeding alone was enough to kill her. And if by some chance, she did recover she would never walk again. Coming to terms with her shattered Olympic dreams and refusing to believe what expert medical staff were telling her about her chances of any kind of recovery, Janine focused every sinew of her being on healing her broken body and crushed morale. Her fighting spirit was rekindled by watching small planes fly overhead. She said to herself 'If I can't walk, I'll fly'. And fly she did. Within a year she had her private pilot's licence. Twelve months later she had her commercial licence, and then her instructor's permit. While she was standing telling her story, I noticed that she kept swaying side-to-side. Her legs were not perfect, but she was still standing and she was still living.

'Dare to Dream' is a significant saying in my life. Without a dream you don't have anything to aspire to. I am a real dreamer and sometimes it is hard to stop thinking about what my next venture will be. If I have a dream, I go for it. I am not scared to fail!

You've had over 18 years of experience in business. Was it all smooth sailing or a bit of a roller-coaster ride?

Having been in business for so long, I guess it seems more like a roller-coaster ride. In the beginning, finding the right job was so hard. I had some great jobs, but then I would get bored because they lacked the challenge. Why? I think I simply hadn't found what I really wanted to do.

Two years ago when I took the first step to start my own business, I was extremely scared. I left a corporate job and started the business with my laptop and a mobile phone – I didn't even have business cards. But I never thought I couldn't do it. I just had to put my mind to it and do some planning, although I didn't really know what that planning was. Business Women Connect has turned out to be exactly what I was looking for. Yes, it is a roller-coaster ride, but it's not a ride I want to hop off in the foreseeable future.

What prompted you to start Business Women Connect (BWC)?

I started BWC because there was a lack of facilities for women on the Central Coast (actually, there was nothing). The idea was developed

tully ©

between my mentor and myself at a luncheon. Christine has supported me from day one and has been like a silent partner, always giving support and advice and asking for nothing in return. I also found that many of the topics being spoken about by speakers at networking functions were very business-oriented, and lacked the ability to inspire people on a personal level as well. So we launched BWC in August 2005 at the Crowne Plaza in Terrigal. Kim Waugh, businesswoman and horse trainer, was our first speaker. My goal was to get 50 people to attend and we ended up with 155. By assessing the response and the type of businesswomen that attended, I knew we were onto a good thing.

What is the philosophy of Business Women Connect?

BWC provides leading businesswomen with the ultimate forum to facilitate business and personal development by networking business-to-business.

This networking opportunity is specifically designed for successful and up-and-coming businesswomen to strive and develop themselves and their businesses. We connect, nurture, and help all women to grow personally and in business. We share knowledge selflessly and share the success with others.

Did you do a lot of research before getting Business Women Connect up and going?

Yes, research for anything is so important. I knew a lot of women in business and started ringing around to see what their thoughts were. They loved the idea of getting together once a month for lunch and receiving some inspiration and business guidance. Based on our launch, it was obvious that the research we had gathered had steered us in the right direction. We now survey regularly to make sure that we haven't lost focus on what we need to do in order to continue providing great service. The business has changed dramatically since its inception and sometimes you need to revisit to get a good perspective on your business.

Can you explain what Business Women Connect does?

BWC provides a forum for women to come together and network, while at the same time listening to great speakers. Networking is the main reason that women come to a breakfast or lunch, in addition to listening to a topical speaker who provides motivational advice on business or personal issues. But it isn't all just about a breakfast, lunch and guest speaker. We are also developing a women's expo to assist women with a range of issues – Business, Mind and Body. And we are developing key ways of recognising regional women in business and will be holding annual Women in Business Awards to recognise these high achievers.

> 66 My goal was to get 50 people to attend and we ended up with 155. 99

What were some of the challenges you faced in the first few months of starting your business? What did you learn from them?

In the first few months, I 'Dared to Dream'. I was trying to sell a dream to sponsors and trying to recruit new members at the same time. But how do you sell your dream to someone when you have no statistics? I was trying to sell something that was yet to exist. I didn't really know how this was going to happen but I told myself that if I needed to get up at 6am and work through to 11pm, then that's the way it needed to be. My part-time assistant started working four days a week so that we could accommodate the business as it was evolving – I quickly learnt that having the right staff, who love your business as much as you do, is a great asset.

Cash flow was another challenge. I was, and still am, hopeless with accounts and financial management. So I had my assistant skilled-up in MYOB and she took over that part of the business (Rhonda is my rock, and the eyes and ears of the business). I was always looking at my systems and working out ways to improve the next luncheon. This also served as a great way to measure our ongoing success. But the hardest thing in the first few months was having people doubt what I was doing, and wishing me luck instead. I didn't need luck – I needed their commitment. At the end of the day, I believed in what I was doing and this was confirmed by the responses of the businesswomen turning up each month to be motivated and inspired.

Having had many great speakers share their wisdom at your events, what are some of the key ideas and messages that have stuck with you?

No matter which speakers we invite or what background they come from, there is one common message that has stuck with me – 'have a go!'

One speaker I will never forget was Nancy Bird-Walton, the first female aviator. She was 91 years old and stood on stage with such grace and admiration for all of the other successful businesswomen in the room. What this woman did for aviation history was amazing. What a life she had lived, and the changes to women's rights she witnessed over the years were just incredible. When she flew, aviation was still in its infancy and fraught with many dangers and difficulties – mechanical problems, frail aeroplanes made of fabric and wood, dust storms, poor or no aviation maps, and sketchy weather reports that would often turn a flight into a test of courage and perseverance. Her key message was that if she didn't have the drive and determination to fly, she wouldn't have done it.

I only hope that when I am 91 I look as good as Nancy Bird-Walton and have experienced at least half the life of this wonderful and inspiring woman.

What are the three different types of networkers?

Passive networkers – these people do this on a regular basis. They won't push their products or services but they will certainly make themselves known to you. They sit on the edge of the room and watch everyone come in the door. They wait to be approached and if they get work out of the day, it's a bonus.

Assertive networkers – these people love to network and catch up with people they know and want to get to know. They don't push their products or services but they certainly let you know what they do (they have business cards on them at all times). These people are relationship-building people and are not purely networking to get a sale. They believe in the laws of attraction – what you give out, you will receive in return. If they say they will do something, they do it. These are people you need to get to know.

66 If they say they will do something, they do it. These are people you need to get to know. 99

Serial networkers – these people network at any function that they can get leads from. They tend to be quite pushy and will meet as many people in the room as possible and will collect as many business cards as they can. They will make appointments to follow up on conversations and they will usually hound you until they get an outcome.

Can you offer some tips to people who want to start or have just started networking?

- *Business cards* – have professionally-designed and printed business cards.
- *Give without expectation* – do things for others without receiving anything in return.
- *Competitors* – seek opportunities from your competitors.
- *Names* – always make a mental note of people's names (*hint:* say their name three times in a conversation as you will be more likely to remember it).
- *Functions* – be strategic in which networks work best for your business.
- *Sell* – don't hard sell to people you have just met.
- *Relationships* – build relationships with other networkers on a personal and business basis.
- *Meet and greet* – make sure you meet and greet at least five people at any given function (don't make the mistake of getting caught with the one person for too long).
- *Confidence* – fake it until you make it. If you are nervous, tell the host so that they can introduce you to others in the network.
- *Body language* – maintain good posture, don't fidget and wear the appropriate clothing.
- *Introduction* – have a 15 to 30-second introduction about yourself (short and sweet).
- *Listen* – listen to what others have to say.
- *Handshake* – always shake hands with a woman or a man.
- *Kiss* – to kiss or not to kiss? Assess each occasion as it happens.

In what ways has communication been a key factor in your success?

The most important thing I've learnt about communication is to be yourself. Don't be someone you are not. I naturally love to talk and I talk to hundreds of different people each month. Unfortunately, I am not very good with remembering names, so I love business cards with photos on them. I am also inclined to leave a lasting impression on the people I meet, so to be remembered I often wear strong colours and connect with them in a personal, yet topical conversation. But perhaps the key to successful communication is that you deliver on your promises. I insist on doing that. I try to clarify any requirement within a 24-hour timeframe, so it is still in the forefront of that person's mind. There is nothing better than a quick response from someone.

What would be your top seven tips to improve the way in which you communicate with others?

I have hundreds of tips on communication strategies for people in business. Here are some of the key principles that I follow.

- *Listen* – remember that you have one mouth and two ears.
- *Authenticity* – don't put on a show and brag about yourself, people will see straight through it.
- *Confidence* – have just enough confidence to get your message across, but don't be too assertive.
- *Promise* – if you promise someone something, make sure you deliver it.
- *Follow up* – when you meet people either follow up with a phone call or email saying it was nice to meet them and that you look forward to meeting again.
- *Personal interests* – find out what personal interests people have, and don't always talk about work.
- *Empathy* – understand and have compassion.

How has being an avid goal setter helped you over the years?

My goal setting technique is very visual – I need to see what I am doing, where I am going and what I am working for. I have a whiteboard in my office that I glance at about 30 to 40 times a day. This is a constant visual reminder of where the business is going and why I am in it. I see it, I think it and it happens!

Setting goals over the years has helped me tremendously. When setting goals, make both personal and business goals. The personal goals will make you feel great, which in turn will allow your business goals to become reality. When I started the business I owned a house with my ex-husband. My goal was for my business to make enough money within 18 months for me to purchase his share of the house. I was so focused on the goal of getting my house back that the business made enough money and now I wholly own my house.

What are some of your goals for the next five years?

My personal goal is to find a solution to the work/life balance option. Like most people, I struggle with this every day. Having a business that is still very young I want to put my energy into it all the time. It is so easy to go to work to type a quick email and find yourself there three hours later, still doing work. I now insist on weekends with my family and that might mean that during the week I need to start work at 7.00am instead of 8.30am in order to get the work done.

There are three types of goals that I set:

- *Personal goals* – currently I am focusing on weight-loss and improving my sense of betterment as a person from the inside.
- *Short-term goals* – these are daily goals that I set to ensure that I have accomplished something for the day. For example, to obtain two media hits for the business during the week I might write a media release,

email it out, and follow it up. These are achievable goals that I can fulfil short term.

• *Long-term business goals* – these are goals that will require a bit more time to achieve. My current long-term goal is to achieve national branding in regional areas for BWC.

Over the next five years, BWC will continue to grow, with plans to increase our membership base from 210 to 1,000. My intention is to have over 5,000 members by the end of 2009. Depending on the success of this expansion, I will consider a franchise or licence arrangement with local key businesspeople throughout the country. Tied in with my business goals, I also have a personal goal of embracing public speaking opportunities to promote networking and marketing philosophies to a wider audience.

Over the next three to five years I see the networking and business relationships industry expanding rapidly through face-to-face interaction and online product offerings. BWC currently offers a premium service to five regional areas around Sydney – Wollongong, St George/Sutherland, the Central Coast, Newcastle/Hunter and Port Stephens – and has gone through sufficient learning to expand to other regions. A key growth initiative for BWC is offering products suitable for women in business, and not just networking events. The products are chosen based upon the ability of the product to educate and support women in their business decision processes. However, the main goal is to have our traditional marketing, e-marketing and website systems all aligned. This will allow BWC to strengthen its online presence in a professional and economic manner, thus generating a stronger return on our investment.

What do you see as the biggest challenge facing young women today and what can we do about it?

The biggest challenge for women today is self-belief: I can't do that; I won't get that promotion; I don't know how to run

66 My personal goal is to find a solution to the work/life balance option. 99

a business! If you think you can't, you won't be able to do anything. The mind is such a powerful instrument and keeping positive about myself is something that I work on every day. I am a very positive person, but I still work on it. If I feel down (and jeez, there are times when I get down), I distract myself with a reward – usually shopping for shoes or chocolate.

Women have limited career opportunities in the workplace and research proves that fewer women hold employment in high corporate positions. Women who receive these opportunities need to appreciate their achievement and encourage other women to aspire to similar positions or successes. This can be done through mentoring programs, education, training, and the self-belief that they can do it. And what about juggling families and careers? Women with families face another set of challenges to say the least. The good thing to note is that women are becoming more independent. Keeping this in mind, I believe there is an ever-important need to educate young girls and women to feel better about themselves. It starts at home, then school, then work, then through their children. We can all help someone to make a difference.

What advice would you give to women making important career decisions?

When making career decisions follow your head and your heart. Do all the necessary research to ensure that your decision can lead to success and that it is realistic and attainable for you. Believe in who you are and what you are capable of. Have no self-doubt and enjoy the ride of success!

How has Business Women Connect grown and what are your plans for the future?

BWC has grown over one-and-a-half years, from our first launch in the Central Coast in 2005 to our fifth launch in the Illawarra region in 2006. By June 2007, BWC will be in another three regions so this will make a total of eight regional areas for women to network their business in. Our plans for the future include women's expos, awards events, and franchising and licencing opportunities. We want to connect women in regional areas and be an advocate for other women's networks across the country.

What do you love most about being where you are today?

What I love about where I am today is that I am succeeding in my chosen field. I love my work and I love the women that I am surrounded with every day. I have the ability to work from a home-based office, which is rather funny as most people assume that we have a fancy office in a prestigious location. Perception is great but the reality is that it's convenient. Cooper is now in high school and having the flexibility of being there for him is really good. I love that I now have the opportunity to help other women get started in their businesses and to connect them with other like-minded businesses. There are wonderful programs on mentoring, business development, cash flow, having the right insurances, and much more that we can educate them in. We now help facilitate these avenues for women in business and that is so rewarding. When I wake-up every morning, I get butterflies in my stomach from the excitement of going to work – most people working corporate jobs would think I'm mad!

At the end of your life how do you want to be remembered?

This is a really hard question. I want to be remembered as a person who tried and succeeded. If I look back on my life, would I have done anything differently? The answer would be no. Life takes you on a journey for different learning experiences and gives you outcomes from those experiences. My path has been created by the opportunities I have chosen to take, and the people I have met have come into my life for a reason. I hope that people remember me as someone who helped them personally and professionally, without any expectation of receiving something in return. I hope people say that I was sharing, loving, caring and always offered a strong and supportive opinion – and served as an inspiration to businesswomen!

FINAL THOUGHTS

We imagine that your head is probably spinning with a multitude of thoughts and different emotions right now. What these inspirational women have made seem so simple can actually be quite complex when you delve beneath the surface and start to pull it all apart. Hopefully though, the overriding emotion is one of inspiration and a feeling that you too are capable of achieving great success.

Despite the title of this book, there really is no great secret to living an inspirational life. As this book demonstrates, all the information you will ever require to succeed is freely available, as long as you have the drive, courage and 'smarts' to actively seek out what you need to know.

However, the real driver of success is simply *implementation* – the ability to put into practise, and take action on the things you hear and read. After years of working with people we have seen that this rarely happens by simply reading something once. It comes from re-reading, reflecting and then applying – not just once but until it becomes a habit and part of your life.

With this in mind our strongest recommendation is that you do this exercise: re-read each of the chapters of this book, and with a notepad and pen by your side, write your answers to these two questions:

- What are the three most important things I've learnt from this chapter?
- How can I implement these learnings into my life, starting today?

Yes, we know that it is going to take some time, but as they say, the only place where success comes before work is in the dictionary. And we are not talking about physical work, a bit of solid thinking is all it takes. So give it a try, after a few short weeks you'll be amazed at the impact it will have.

Also, as we said in the preface of this book, you are your most valuable asset so make sure you keep investing in yourself. That is why we have provided the many bonuses for you. Make sure you go to the webpage (that's if you haven't already) and download all of the gifts. They contain some fantastic material which you will wholeheartedly enjoy.

In closing, remember this: 'Nobody can go back to the beginning and make a brand new start. But everyone can start from now and make a brand new end', so begin on your path now! Don't worry about the past, and don't worry that you don't know enough – you probably never will. Just make a start, begin on your path today and continue learning as you go.

We trust that you've enjoyed this book. It has been a real honour to work with these amazing women and to share their stories. Take their ideas to heart, put them into action and watch your dreams soar.

DREAM BIG!

Dale Beaumont and Emma Lyons

P.S. For anyone either looking to start their own business, or already doing it, we strongly suggest also reading *Secrets of Female Entrepreneurs Exposed!* This book provides even more invaluable insights from 17 highly successful businesswomen, sharing hundreds of business-building ideas and more great strategies for a happy and successful life.

Other 'Secrets Exposed!' Books Available Now

Secrets of Male Entrepreneurs Exposed!

Secrets of Property Millionaires Exposed!

Secrets of Female Entrepreneurs Exposed!

Secrets of Young Achievers Exposed!

Secrets of Small Business Owners Exposed!

Secrets of Great Public Speakers Exposed!

Other 'Secrets Exposed!' Books Launching 2007

Secrets of Entrepreneurs Under 40 Exposed!

Secrets of Inspiring Leaders Exposed!

Secrets of Great Success Coaches Exposed!

Secrets of Top Sales Professionals Exposed!

Secrets of Internet Entrepreneurs Exposed!

Secrets of Marketing Experts Exposed!

Secrets of Top Business Builders Exposed!

Secrets of Winning Franchises Exposed!

Secrets of Great Company CEOs Exposed!

For the latest information on the release of the above
'Secrets Exposed!' books, please visit:

www.SecretsExposed.com.au or **www.DaleBeaumont.com**

How to claim your *free* bonus gift...

Some of our contributors have generously offered FREE bonus gifts to all our readers. Here are some of the things you'll receive simply by visiting our website:

FREE GIFT # 1 **($19.95 Value) The Art Of Powerful Living** – Over the last ten years Rosie Pekar has made her mark as the world's best But-Kicker. In this delightful e-book you'll receive inspirational ideas that you'll need to discover the path to taking control of your life. Packed with dozens of tips and notable quotes that will focus your mind, you'll learn the art of powerful living.

FREE GIFT # 2 **($29.95 Value) 50 Ways To Find More Money!** – Cydney O'Sullivan is a successful businesswoman, investor and single mother of two. Having started her first business in her early twenties, Cydney has gone on to develop numerous companies and a multimillion-dollar real estate and share portfolio. Now on a mission to help other women, Cydney has designed a fun and creative e-book full of ideas for finding more cash and securing your own financial future.

FREE GIFT # 3 **($14.95 Value) A Collection of Inspirational Quotes** – Miriam has been an avid collector of quotes for most of her life. In this wonderful e-book she has compiled some of the most heart-warming quotes written by the world's most gifted writers. Guaranteed to uplift your spirit, the wisdom they contain will inspire new thoughts and light the path to greater happiness and fulfilment.

FREE GIFT # 4 **($49.50 Value) Everything You Always Wanted To Know About How To Get A Life** – Life Balancing expert, Jennifer Jefferies has taught some of the world's leading corporations how to help their staff to 'get a life'. With

Simply visit the special web page below and
follow the directions to download your free gifts:

www.SecretsExposed.com.au/inspiring-women

...valued at over $247

her 7 Steps to Sanity®, Jennifer has a prescription for modern living. In this no-nonsense and no-guilt-trip e-book, Jennifer will help you incorporate these powerful strategies into your everyday life. So start reading today and lead a more balanced, energised and happy life.

FREE GIFT # 5 ($19.95 Value) Event-Specific Networking – In this special collection of articles, businesswoman and networking specialist Kim McGuinness shares a host of valuable tips to maximise your value and effectiveness when attending any function or event. By learning these powerful life skills, not only will you be able to create memorable interactions, but you'll learn to capitalise on those connections for mutual benefit.

FREE GIFT # 6 ($19.95 Value) The Entrepreneurial Mother's Guide To Working Out What You Want – Denise Hall is the director of aCE talentNET which focuses on performance improvement. As her company is run almost entirely by entrepreneurial women, she has collected a host of tried and tested strategies designed to help working women maximise their productivity, while at the same time creating a better quality of life. Formatted as a handy workbook, this bonus will not only benefit you but those around you as well.

FREE GIFT # 7 ($100.00 Value) Four Key Guiding Principals Of Living An Empowered Life – Sally Anderson truly has been to hell and back, however she managed to turn an extremely negative experience into a positive one, becoming a Legacy Coach and guiding people through life and all its challenges. This downloadable audio presentation speaks of the four guiding principles of living an empowered life. If you knew how to live a life where you always felt empowered, what could you accomplish?

---

* The *free* bonus gifts offered by contributors are current at the time of printing. If a particular gift is no longer available, we will substitute another gift of similar value and content. For the most up-to-date information please visit www.SecretsExposed.com.au/inspiring-women.

** The intellectual property rights (including trademarks and copyrights) associated with each of the bonus gifts offered are those of the respective creators. Unauthorised distribution, modification or copying of any of these documents is prohibited without the express written permission of the creators.

About the authors

Dale Beaumont

Dale Beaumont was born in Sydney in June 1981. Growing up, he participated in a number of sports and at the age of nine was selected for the elite NSW Gymnastics Squad. Training 34 hours per week, he soon learnt the value of discipline, hard work, having a coach and most importantly, delayed gratification.

After six years of intensive training, Dale changed his sporting focus to competitive aerobics so that he could spend more time on his studies and pursue other interests. In 1998 he became the National Aerobics Champion and the youngest Australian to compete at the World Aerobics Championships, where he placed eighth.

After finishing high school, Dale began attending various personal development and success seminars, where he learnt from people such as Jim Rohn, Michael Rowland, Bob Proctor, Robert Kiyosaki, John Maxwell, Brandon Bays, Brad Sugars, Mark Victor Hanson and many others.

At the age of 19, together with good friend Brent Williams, Dale wrote his first book titled *The World at Your Feet*, and co-founded Tomorrow's Youth International, which now runs educational and self-development programs for 13 to 21-year-olds in four countries. Dale has been featured on the *Today* show, *Sunrise*, *Mornings with Kerri-Anne*, as well as in countless newspapers and magazines.

Most recently, Dale has been hard at work developing the 'Secrets Exposed' series, to bring together the very best material from hundreds of Australasia's most successful people. With more than twenty books planned for the next three years and an up-coming seminar series, Dale is now a sought-after speaker on topics such as: start-up business, networking skills, book publishing, internet marketing and generating publicity.

Dale lives in Sydney with his beautiful and very supportive wife, Katherine. With a baby next on the 'to-do' list and lots of international travel plans, Dale is looking forward to the challenges ahead, and to spending more time enjoying life.

For more information about Dale's workshops and educational materials, or to book him as a guest speaker at your next conference or event, please visit:
www.DaleBeaumont.com

Emma Lyons

Emma Lyons was born in 1984 in Auckland, New Zealand. Being an only child, she always enjoyed the company of her very supportive and successful parents, Kathy and Geoff. From an early age she knew that she wanted to work in the communications industry and tailored her schoolwork to reflect this goal.

Once finishing high school she set her sights on a Bachelor of Communications in Auckland, and once accepted, developed her love for journalism. During this time she wrote numerous articles for a variety of newspapers and magazines. After three years she completed her degree and took up a position at ACP Media.

As a freelance journalist, she felt that her passion was not being fulfilled (and her wallet certainly wasn't either). Ready for a new adventure, she applied for an exciting but possibly unrealistic position, which was across the Tasman. She was offered the role and although she had no previous plans to relocate, within two weeks she was on a plane with the support of her family and friends.

Emma is now the project manager for the 'Secrets Exposed' series and believes that her move to Sydney was the best thing she has ever done. One of her lifelong goals was to become a published author and she is thrilled to have achieved this at such a young age.

When she is not working (which at the moment is hardly ever), Emma enjoys reading, cooking, travel and exploring the nightlife of her new city.

About our contributors

We would again like to say a huge 'thank you' to the amazing speakers who have helped to make this book possible. Many of them have their own books and other educational products – for more information, feel free to contact them directly.

Rosie Pekar – Butkicking Enterprises
Address: PO Box 1203 Broadbeach QLD 4218
Phone: 0407 004 294
Email: rosie@kickbut.com.au   Website: **www.kickbut.com.au**
Books: *Time To KickBut®! Facts Of Life… Exposed, Mission Possible*

Mia Freedman – Channel Nine
Address: PO Box 27 Willoughby NSW 2068
Email: mia@miafreedman.com.au   Website & Blog: **www.miafreedman.com.au**
Books: *The New Black*

Terry Hawkins – People In Progress Pty Ltd
Address: PO Box 77 Palm Beach NSW 2108
Phone: (02) 9918 7777   Fax: (02) 9918 7755
Email: mail@peopleinprogress.com.au
Websites: **www.peopleinprogress.com.au** and **www.terryhawkins.com.au**
Books: *There Are Only Two Times In Life… Now Or Too Late, Stickman Rules! Children's Book Series, The Power Of More Than One – Collaboration Of Leading Business And Motivational Speakers*

Lauren Burns – Lauren Burns Pty Ltd
Address: PO Box 1229 Fitzroy North VIC 3068
Email: info@laurenburns.com   Website: **www.laurenburns.com.au**
Books: *Fighting Spirit*

Lisa McInnes-Smith – Smart Choices
Address: PO Box 2589 Cheltenham VIC 3192
Phone: (03) 9585 2399   Fax: (03) 9583 0221
Email: lisa@lisaspeaks.com   Website: **www.lisaspeaks.com**
Books: *Why Wasn't I Told?, How To Motivate Manage and Market Yourself, Keeping Couples Cooking, How To Build A Better Life*

Cydney O'Sullivan – Ms Independence Pty Ltd
Phone: 1300 BE RICH
Email: secrets@msindependence.com   Website: **www.msindependence.com**
Books: *Rich Girls Have More Shoes – 101 Staggeringly Simple Steps To Money Mastery*

Miriam Schafer – Holistic Life Coach
Address: Noosa Heads QLD
Phone: (07) 5455 4550   Fax: (07) 5455 4551
Email: mjs888@optusnet.com.au   Website: **www.miriamschafer.com**

Jo Cowling
Email: jo@jolosingit.com   Website: **www.jolosingit.com**

Jennifer Jefferies – Jennifer Jefferies International
Address: PO Box 4298 Elanora QLD 4221
Phone: (07) 5598 6035   Fax: (07) 5598 6036
Email: jennifer@jenniferjefferies.com   Website: **www.jenniferjefferies.com**
Books: *The 7 Steps To Sanity®, Sanity Savers, Calm Kids*

Kim McGuinness – Network Central
Address: PO Box 334 Pymble BC NSW 2073
Phone: 1300 667 075   Fax: 1300 667 465
Email: info@networkcentral.com.au   Website: **www.networkcentral.com.au**
Books: *Network Or Perish – Learn The Secrets Of Master Networkers*

Denise Hall – aCE talentNET
Address: 126 Fordham Ave Camberwell VIC 3124
Phone: (03) 9889 5317   Fax: (03) 9889 5314
Email: theentrepreneurialmother@acetalentnet.com.au
Website: **www.theentrepreneurialmother.com.au** and **www.acetalentnet.com.au**

Sally Anderson – Sally Anderson Limited
Address: PO Box 91770 AMSC Auckland New Zealand
Phone: (+649) 360 7298   Fax: (+649) 360 7297
Email: sal@sallyanderson.co.nz   Website: **www.sallyanderson.co.nz**

Simone Preston – Business Women Connect
Address: PO Box 679 Terrigal NSW 2260
Phone: (02) 4385 8529   Fax: (02) 4385 8439
Email: info@businesswomenconnect.com.au
Website: **www.businesswomenconnect.com.au**

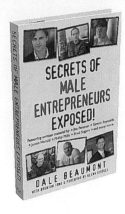
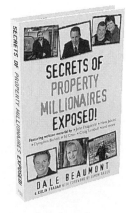

Secrets of Female Entrepreneurs Exposed!

In this book you'll discover...

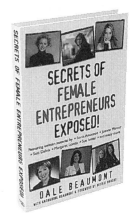

- The skills of starting and running your own business
- How to establish your client base and deliver a professional service
- The secrets of networking and creating business partnerships
- Creative tips for finding and training your team
- How to receive media publicity and lots of free advertising
- What you need to do to expand your business ideas around the world
- How to effectively balance business success and family life

Featuring written material by...

Sonia Amoroso (Cat Media) • **Joanne Mercer** (Joanne Mercer Footwear) • **Sue Ismiel** (Nad's Hair Removal) • **Carol Comer** (High Impact Marketing) • **Sue Whyte** (Intimo Lingerie) • **Kristina Noble & Simone Babic** (Citrus Internet) • **Sandy Forster** (Wildly Wealthy Women) • **Katrina Allen** (DeJour) • **Suzi Dafnis** (Pow Wow Events) • **Tanya Bension** (Corporate Training Australia) • **Amy Lyden** (Bow Wow Meow) • **Margaret Lomas** (Destiny Group) • **Suzy Yates** (Baystreet Mediaworks) • **Kristina Karlsson** (kikki. K) • **Shelley Barrett** (ModelCo.) • **Kirsty Dunphey** (M&M Harcourts)

Secrets of Young Achievers Exposed!

In this book you'll discover...

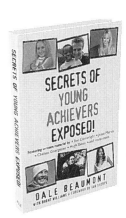

- What it takes to become a real success
- How to know what you want to do with your life
- How to get motivated and stay motivated
- How to overcome criticism and discouragement
- What all super-achievers have in common
- How to reach the top of any career, *fast*
- How to turn your dream into reality

Featuring written material by...

Bec Hewitt (Celebrity Actress) • **Jesse Martin** (Young Adventurer) • **Chelsea Georgeson** (Pro Surfer) • **Amy Wilkins** (TV Presenter & Fitness Coach) • **Hugh Evans** (Community & Aid Worker) • **Ilona Novacek** (Leading Model) • **Ben Korbel** (International DJ) • **Stephanie Williams** (Ballet Dancer) • **Tim Goodwin** (Aboriginal Activist) • **Simon Tedeschi** (Concert Pianist) • **Torah Bright** (Pro Snowboarder) • **Jeremy Lim** (Singaporean Ambassador)

www.SecretsExposed.com.au

Free CD and guide to help you discover how to publish your own book and become a best-selling author

Would you like to sky-rocket your credibility, be seen as an expert in your field and open up doorways to publicity that others can only dream about? Then it is probably time you wrote your own book...

After receiving hundreds of calls and emails, best-selling author Dale Beaumont decided to create a range of resources to help other aspiring authors, and reveal everything you need to know to write, publish and market your own best-selling book.

Starting with a *free* 68-minute Audio CD and a 43-page Publishing Guide (valued at $147) you'll discover…

- The 7 quickest and easiest ways to get your book published.

- Over a dozen costly mistakes that 98% of new authors make and how you can avoid them.

- What every author should know about major publishers, specialised publishers, literary agents, self-publishing and vanity publishers before trying to get published.

- Why co-authoring a book can double your chances of getting published.

- The correct royalty percentage that every author should be paid, so you don't get paid less than what you deserve.

- Why hiring the right vanity publisher almost guarantees your book will be published, but the wrong one can send you broke. Learn where to find the credible ones.

- Should you self-publish your book? Discover the pros and cons about publishing and self-publishing before you make this vital decision.

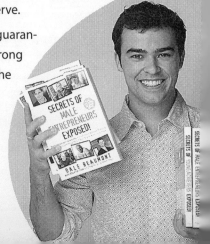

And the best part is, this information is written in *plain english*, so you do not need any previous book publishing experience or prior knowledge to understand it!

"Whether you are a fiction, non-fiction or even a poetry writer, Dale Beaumont will change the way you think about publishing – forever! Absorb his wisdom and follow his plan."

Dan Poynter *(World's Leading Self-Publishing Expert and Author of over 100 books)*

"Dale's information has equipped me with all the nuts and bolts on how to become an author, not just dream about it! Thanks Dale for your genuine passion for publishing and generosity in sharing it with us. I guarantee you will be mentioned in my first book!"

Yang Suk Jung

"Without a doubt, Dale is one of the most informed people in the world when it comes to book publishing. Having Dale's information will literally guarantee your success as a publisher."

John Bertone *(Businessman and author of* Mobile Phone Secrets)

"I'm blown-away with the amount of information being given so openly and freely. I discovered that you don't need years of study in publishing to get started. The information provided is sufficient to get out there and get my books out. Thank you for taking the time to share. I recommend this information to anyone because it helps to totally eliminate the fear of publishing."

Gaz Lowe *(Author of* Whispers of the Real Heart)

Whether you have already had your book rejected by a mainstream publisher, or you have an idea but are yet to get started…you'll get the information you'll need to get into print *fast!*

To download your *free* 68-minute Audio CD and 43-page Publishing Guide (valued at $147) today simply visit the following website…

www.GetPublishedSecrets.com

Discover the amazing success behind Australia's leading educational and 'life-skills' program for teenagers and young adults

After five years and more than 7,300 thrilled participants in four countries, your teenager *now* has the opportunity to experience the highly acclaimed 2½ day advanced life-skills seminar *'Empower-U'*...

- Do you feel that your teenager could be achieving more, but can't seem to get them motivated?
- Do you want to give them the *best* education possible?
- Do you want them to have every means at their disposal to live a happy, successful and rewarding life?

Then you need to discover *why* thousands of parents agree that the 2½ day *'Empower U'* program is the best decision you can make for your son or daughter's future…

In a fun, teenager-friendly environment, Dale Beaumont and Brent Williams will reveal the very same motivation and high-achievement secrets that propel the world's top performers to success – and that are already working wonders for thousands of kids across Australia. Secrets that your child will learn and apply to their life immediately. Secrets we've made so simple to understand and use that you will notice *immediate improvements*.

At *Empower U* your child will become so motivated, so focused, and so determined to succeed that they could well become a super-achiever in a very short time. Your child will walk away from *Empower U* with total *belief* in their own abilities and absolute *certainty* that they can achieve anything they want. Plus, they will have a 'toolkit' full of specific strategies they can use to convert their desires into tangible, real-world results – starting right away!

It doesn't matter whether your child just needs some friendly encouragement or a total 'attitude overhaul', *Empower U* will give them the belief, tools and strategies they need to get moving in the right direction.

"I am so glad that a friend told me about Empower U. My daughter attended almost two years ago at the age of fourteen. She is now seventeen and more motivated than ever. I think the most amazing thing about her experience is that it was not just a one-off. They have supported her the whole way and that has been just terrific."

Peter Stacey   *(Father of Jessica)*

"Empower U was absoultely awesome! *I have never truly learned, enjoyed and been touched by something as much as this in my whole life. I think this program will significantly impact on my future in a positive note and I can never express my gratitude enough."*

Sameer Chowdhury   (Age 17)

"My two daughters attended the Empower U program. One excited, one sceptical. The change in both of them is truly amazing. I am now such a big fan and I just hope that more people take the chance on this that I did. Because then they will see what I now see."

Tura Lechminka   *(Mother of Alana and Kathryn)*

Whether it's more motivation, improved attitude, better exam marks, a savings plan, landing a great job, or just a more open family relationship… you will see results *fast!*

To enrol your son or daughter into the next *Empower U* program simply give us a call or check out our website…

Tomorrow's Youth International
1300 732 782
www.TomorrowsYouth.com.au